TEAM USA & FIFA WORLD CUP
WORKBOOK

FUN ACTIVITIES FOR SOCCER ENTHUSIASTES

© Okyere Bonna, MBA

authorHOUSE®

AuthorHouse™
1663 Liberty Drive
Bloomington, IN 47403
www.authorhouse.com
Phone: 1-800-839-8640

First published by AuthorHouse   [06/06/2011]

ISBN: 978-1-4634-1929-5 (sc)
ISBN: 978-1-4634-1930-1 (ebk)

Printed in the United States of America

Any people depicted in stock imagery provided by Thinkstock are models, and such images are being used for illustrative purposes only.
Certain stock imagery © Thinkstock.

This book is printed on acid-free paper.

Table of contents

LESSON 1
Timothy Matthew Howard

Answer Key 0380590
Word Bank

an	it	quite
for	parents	

Directions: Fill in each blank with a word from the word bank that best completes the story.

Born of mixed-race *(1) RNSATEP* _____, Tim Howard showed *(2) AN* _____ aptitude for football *(3) TQUIE* _____ early, and coupled *(4) IT* _____ with his penchant *(5) FRO* _____ basketball, the goalkeeper position seemed a perfect fit for the athletic youngster.

(Answer ID # 0380590)

1.	2.	3.
_____	_____	_____
4.	5.	
_____	_____	

Answer Key 0828026

Directions: Fill in each blank with a word from the word bank that best completes the story and copy your answers in space provided

Tim Howard's parents divorced *(1)* _ _ _ _ _ he was three *(2)* _ _ _ _ _ _ old, and Howard *(3)* _ _ _ _ _ _ with his mother, *(4)* _ project manager for a *(5)* _ _ _ _ _ _ _ _ _ _ distributor. Though a long-distance *(6)* _ _ _ _ _ _ driver for a *(7)* _ _ _ _ _ _ _ care firm Tim *(8)* _ _ _ _ _ _ _ _ _ father maintained a *(9)* _ _ _ _ _ _ _ _ _ in his life *(10)* _ _ _ got Howard and *(11)* _ _ _ brother, Chris, involved *(12)* _ _ sports. Before Tim Howard *(13)* _ _ _ _ _ _ walk, his father *(14)* _ _ _ _ _ _ _ him equipment for *(15)* _ _ _ _ _ _ _ _ sports to see *(16)* _ _ _ _ _ games he preferred. *(17)* _ _ _ showed a preference *(18)* _ _ _ basketball and soccer. Tim *(19)* _ _ _ _ _ _ _ was diagnosed with *(20)* _ _ _ _ _ _ _ _ _ syndrome when he *(21)* _ _ _ in the sixth *(22)* _ _ _ _ _ _. Howard's rise to the *(23)* _ _ _ tier of European *(24)* _ _ _ _ football with Everton and for *(25)* _ _ _ US national team *(26)* _ _ _ been nothing short *(27)* _ _ meteoric.

(Answer ID # 0828026)

1.	2.	3.
4.	5.	6.
7.	8.	9.
10.	11.	12.
13.	14.	15.
16.	17.	18.
19.	20.	21.
22.	23.	24.
25.	26.	27.

Answer Key 1032958
Word Bank

Howard	club	his	truck
Howard's	cosmetics	in	various
Tim	could	lived	was
Tourette	for	of	when
a	grade	presence	which
and	has	the	years
bought	health	top	

Directions: Fill in each blank with a word from the word bank that best completes the story and copy your answers in space provided

Tim Howard's parents divorced *(1) NEWH* _____ he was three *(2) SEYAR* _____ old, and Howard *(3) VDELI* _____ with his mother, *(4) A* _____ project manager for a *(5) CTOSEICSM* _____ distributor.

Though a long-distance *(6) CUKTR* _____ driver for a *(7) HHLTAE* _____ care firm Tim *(8) OS'DRAHW* _____ father maintained a *(9) ECSENEPR* _____ in his life *(10) NAD* _____ got Howard and *(11) SIH* _____ brother, Chris, involved *(12) IN* _____ sports.

Before Tim Howard *(13) LCDOU* _____ walk, his father *(14) BHGOUT* _____ him equipment for *(15) SOURAVI* _____ sports to see *(16) HCHIW* _____ games he preferred. *(17) MIT* _____ showed a preference *(18) FRO* _____ basketball and soccer. Tim *(19) AORDWH* _____ was diagnosed with *(20) ERETTUTO* _____ syndrome when he *(21) SAW* _____ in the sixth *(22) DREAG* _____. Howard's rise to the *(23) TPO* _____ tier of European *(24) BCLU* _____ football with Everton and for *(25) EHT* _____ US national team *(26) SAH* _____ been nothing short *(27) OF* _____ meteoric.

(Answer ID # 1032958)

1.	2.	3.
4.	5.	6.
7.	8.	9.
10.	11.	12.
13.	14.	15.
16.	17.	18.
19.	20.	21.
22.	23.	24.
25.	26.	27.

Answer Key 0982687
Word Bank

Bulls)	as	head	the
Howard	at	helm	to
Howard's	athleticism	hit	up
MLS's	attention	in	was
Manchester	becoming	long-term	week
MetroStars	career	lower	where
Red	clubs	made	with
Soccer	do	manager	won
Tim	fans	national	year
United	football's	native	youngest
a	for	of	
abilities	further	status	

Directions: Fill in each blank with a word from the word bank that best completes the story and copy your answers in space provided.

After a short (1) REERCA _____ in the USA's (2) RWLEO _____ leagues in his (3) IVTEAN _____ New Jersey in 1998, (4) ITM _____ Howard was snapped (5) UP _____ by the MetroStars (now (6) HTE _____ New York Red (7) SB)LUL _____ of Major League (8) CRCSOE _____.
Almost at once (9) IN _____ 1998, Tim Howard became (10) A _____ crucial member of the (11) RTTSAORSEM _____ (now the New York (12) DER _____ Bulls), earning fan-favorite (13) TSSAUT _____ for his incredible (14) HIIEATSCMLT _____ and shot-stopping ability.
Tim (15) DAOHWR _____, the net-minder, earned (16) UTREHRF _____ plaudits in 2001 when, (17) AT _____ 22, he became the (18) UOEGNYST _____ ever winner of (19) LS'MS _____ goalkeeper of the (20) AEYR _____ award.
Following 2001, Tim (21) WR'HOADS _____ exploits caught the (22) NNTTOIEAT _____ of the decision-makers at the (23) LMEH _____ of United States (24) ILNTAANO _____ team, as well (25) AS _____ Sir Alex Ferguson, (26) EADH _____ coach of Manchester (27) EUDNIT _____, one of world (28) FOLTS'BOLA _____ managerial icons.
In 2003, Tim Howard (29) WSA _____ off to Manchester United, (30) WREEH _____ he stepped in (31) ROF _____ Fabien Barthez in the (32) HTNMRECESA _____ United goal.
Tim Howard (33) LEISABITI _____, honed in MLS, (34) DEAM _____ him an instant (35) IHT _____ with his new (36) EANMARG _____, and he looked (37) TO _____ have found a (38) GELMON-TR _____ home at one (39) OF _____ the world's biggest (40) CUBSL _____ playing in front of 60,000-plus (41) FSNA _____ week in and (42) KWEE _____ out.

7

Tim Howard *(43) OWN* _____ an FA Cup *(44) HTWI* _____ Manchester United in 2004, *(45) OECIMGNB* _____ the first American to the *(46) DO* _____ so.

(Answer ID # 0982687)

1.	2.	3.
4.	5.	6.
7.	8.	9.
10.	11.	12.
13.	14.	15.
16.	17.	18.
19.	20.	21.
22.	23.	24.
25.	26.	27.
28.	29.	30.
31.	32.	33.
34.	35.	36.
37.	38.	39.
40.	41.	42.
43.	44.	45.
46.		

Answer Key 0488529
Word Bank

After	USA's	first	outset
American	Unfortunately	he	respect
Athletes	World	his	stage
Crusade	a	in	such
Everton	after	line	team
Friedel	and	long	that
Goodison	arrival	manager	the
Howard's	at	ministry	truly
League	chance	much-publicized	with
PFA	depart	number	youth
Porto	der	of	
Tim	despite	one	
UEFA	end	opted	

Directions: Fill in each blank with a word from the word bank that best completes the story and copy your answers in space provided.

Tim Howard made *(1)* _____ first appearance for *(2)* _____ senior USA team - *(3)* _____ impressive performances at *(4)* _____ level in 2002 during *(5)* _____ friendly against Ecuador. *(6)* _____ in 2004 Tim Howard's *(7)* _____ mistake in the *(8)* _____ Champions League against *(9)* _____ damaged his confidence *(10)* _____ Ferguson, his couch, *(11)* _____ to relegate the *(12)* _____ to the bench *(13)* _____ being selected in the *(14)* _____ best eleven in his *(15)* _____ season. At the *(16)* _____ of the 2005-2006 English *(17)* _____ campaign, it appeared *(18)* _____ Howard was in *(19)* _____ to take over the *(20)* _____ one spot again *(21)* _____ Manchester United, but the *(22)* _____ of Edwin van *(23)* _____ Sar saw him *(24)* _____ to Everton. At *(25)* _____, Tim Howard made the number *(26)* _____ spot from the *(27)* _____, and earned the *(28)* _____ and faith of *(29)* _____ David Moyes. At *(30)* _____ Park, Tim Howard *(31)* _____ shined with Everton. *(32)* _____ backing up Friedel *(33)* _____ the 2000 Olympic Games *(34)* _____ Sydney, Howard got his *(35)* _____ on the big *(36)* _____ as a member *(37)* _____ the US national *(38)* _____ at the FIFA *(39)* _____ Cup Germany 2006™. Tim *(40)* _____ arrival as the *(41)* _____ first-choice goalkeeper was a *(42)* _____ road though, as *(43)* _____ was up against *(44)* _____ standouts as Keller and *(45)* _____.

Outside the field *(46)* _____ Howard is involved with *(47)* _____ in Action, a *(48)* _____ arm of Campus *(49)* _____ for Christ.

9

(Answer ID # 0488529)

1.	2.	3.
4.	5.	6.
7.	8.	9.
10.	11.	12.
13.	14.	15.
16.	17.	18.
19.	20.	21.
22.	23.	24.
25.	26.	27.
28.	29.	30.
31.	32.	33.
34.	35.	36.
37.	38.	39.
40.	41.	42.
43.	44.	45.
46.	47.	48.
49.		

Answer Key 0594431
Word Bank

Africa	States	goals	their
C	USA	held	threaten
CONCACAF	World	in	tied
Cup	and	Although	time
England	at	man	to
He	back	married	two
In	battling	of	up
Match	but	started	was
Park	down	superb	way
Slovenia	elected	the	with

Directions: Fill in each blank with a word from the word bank that best completes the story and copy your answers in space provided.

Tim Howard is *(1)* _ _ _ _ _ _ _ to Laura Howard *(2)* _ _ _ _ whom he has *(3)* _ _ _ children.
Tim Howard *(4)* _ _ _ _ _ _ _ _ every game for *(5)* _ _ _ USA on their *(6)* _ _ _ to winning the 2007 *(7)* _ _ _ _ _ _ _ _ _ Gold Cup and *(8)* _ _ _ instrumental in the *(9)* _ _ _ _ _ _ reaching the final *(10)* _ _ the 2009 FIFA Confederations *(11)* _ _ _.

Howard put up a *(12)* _ _ _ _ _ _ performance at South *(13)* _ _ _ _ _ _ _ 2010 FIFA World Cup. *(14)* _ _ was the main *(15)* _ _ _ that helped Team *(16)* _ _ _ to the Round of 16. *(17)* _ _ their first battle with *(18)* _ _ _ _ _ _ _ Tim Howard was *(19)* _ _ _ _ _ _ _ _ as Man of the *(20)* _ _ _ _ _.In this duel, USA *(21)* _ _ _ _ 1-1 with England thanks *(22)* _ _ Howards many saves. In *(23)* _ _ _ _ _ _ second match with *(24)* _ _ _ _ _ _ _ _ _ Tim still put *(25)* _ _ a splendid performance *(26)* _ _ _ _ _ _ _ _ he conceded two *(27)* _ _ _ _ _. Team USA fought *(28)* _ _ _ _ _ from two goals *(29)* _ _ _ _ _ to earn a *(30)* _ _ _ _ _ _ _ _ _ 2-2 draw with Slovenia *(31)* _ _ _ keep their FIFA *(32)* _ _ _ _ _ _ Cup™ hopes alive *(33)* _ _ an exciting Group *(34)* _ clash at Ellis *(35)* _ _ _ _.There was still *(36)* _ _ _ _ for Novakovic to *(37)* _ _ _ _ _ _ _ _ _ with a header *(38)* _ _ the other end *(39)* _ _ _ his effort was *(40)* _ _ _ _ comfortably by Howard.

(Answer ID # 0594431)

1.	2.	3.
4.	5.	6.
7.	8.	9.
10.	11.	12.
13.	14.	15.
16.	17.	18.
19.	20.	21.
22.	23.	24.
25.	26.	27.
28.	29.	30.
31.	32.	33.
34.	35.	36.
37.	38.	39.
40.		

LESSON 2
Brad Guzan

Answer Key 0399025			
Word Bank			
Aston	September	in	penalties
At	Stadium	instincts	playing
Brad	USA	international	safe
By	a	last	set-up
Chivas	and	made	spring-loaded
Cup	at	namesake	team
Guatemala	began	national	the
Guzan	cap	of	two
Howard	from	one	was
October	had	outfit	
Queens	his	over	

Directions: Fill in each blank with a word from the word bank that best completes the story and copy your answers in space provided

Brad Guzan hails *(1) MOFR* _____ a Polish-American ancestry. *(2) RDBA* _____ Guzan played for *(3) TEH* _____ Under-18 United States *(4) LIOTANAN* _____ team.
Brad Guzan *(5) ANGEB* _____ his professional career *(6) IN* _____ Los Angeles with *(7) AHISVC* _____ USA. In joining Chivas *(8) ASU* _____, Brad Guzan immediately *(9) MAED* _____ an impact with *(10) IHS* _____ amazing shot-stopping ability, *(11) OGRNAIP-DEDSL* _____ reflexes and cool *(12) TNSTISCIN* _____ between the posts.
Brad *(13) AGZNU* _____ got his first *(14) CPA* _____ for the senior national *(15) TAEM* _____ on February 19, 2006, against *(16) AGAEATLUM* _____.
On November 7, 2007, Brad Guzan *(17) WSA* _____ named MLS Goalkeeper *(18) OF* _____ the Year
Brad Guzan made his *(19) ONTSA* _____ Villa debut in *(20) EMERTEBPS* _____ 2008, in the League *(21) CPU* _____, at home to *(22) ENUQES* _____ Park Rangers. On 27th *(23) EROCTOB* _____ 2009, Guzan saved four *(24) IETPNLESA* _____ in one match, *(25) ENO* _____ in normal time *(26) DNA* _____ three more in *(27) A* _____ penalty shoot-out win *(28) ERVO* _____ Sunderland at the *(29) ASTMUDI* _____ of Light in the *(30) TSLA* _____ 16 of the Carling Cup.

13

(31) BY _____ June 2010 Brad Guzan was *(32) NAGLYPI* _____ as understudy to *(33) NEKMAEAS* _____ and former USA *(34) NNOLRITANETIA* _____ hero, Brad Friedel, *(35) AT* _____ English Premier League *(36) OUFITT* _____ at Aston Villa. *(37) AT* _____ South Africa 2010, Brad Guzan *(38) AHD* _____ established himself as a *(39) AESF* _____ and ready number *(40) WTO* _____, behind Everton's Tim *(41) RWADOH* _____, in Bob Bradley's USA *(42) U-TPSE* _____.

(Answer ID # 0399025) **Brad Guzan**

1.	2.	3.
4.	5.	6.
7.	8.	9.
10.	11.	12.
13.	14.	15.
16.	17.	18.
19.	20.	21.
22.	23.	24.
25.	26.	27.
28.	29.	30.
31.	32.	33.
34.	35.	36.
37.	38.	39.
40.	41.	42.

Answer Key 0493731
Word Bank

Beijing	USA's	himself	team
FIFA	a	in	the
Guzan	all	limited	three
June	and	named	to
Martin	antics	national	was
Olympic	for	number	when
Soccer	goalkeeper	of	youth
South	good	performances	
Southern	had	playing	
USA	has	stand-in	

Directions: Fill in each blank with a word from the word bank that best completes the story and copy your answers in space provided

Brad Guzan spent *(1)* _ _ _ _ _ seasons with the *(2)* _ _ _ _ _ _ _ _ California Major League *(3)* _ _ _ _ _ _ outfit and was *(4)* _ _ _ _ _ the league's best *(5)* _ _ _ _ _ _ _ _ _ _ _ of 2007. Brad Guzan's *(6)* _ _ _ _ _ _ _ _ _ _ _ _ attracted the attention *(7)* _ _ Aston Villa boss *(8)* _ _ _ _ _ _ O'Neill, who swooped *(9)* _ _ for the youngster *(10)* _ _ _ eventually secured him *(11)* _ work permit in *(12)* _ _ _ UK.

Brad Guzan *(13)* _ _ _ _ a part of the *(14)* _ _ _ squad that progressed *(15)* _ _ the final of the 2009 *(16)* _ _ _ _ Confederations Cup in *(17)* _ _ _ _ _ Africa. Although Guzan's *(18)* _ _ _ _ _ _ _ time at the *(19)* _ _ _ _ _ _ _ _ _ level has been *(20)* _ _ _ _ _ _ _ by the evergreen *(21)* _ _ _ _ _ _ _ of Friedel, Guzan *(22)* _ _ _ acquitted himself well *(23)* _ _ _ _ _ called upon. Brad *(24)* _ _ _ _ _ _ had firmly established *(25)* _ _ _ _ _ _ _ _ as an able *(26)* _ _ _ _ _ _ _ _ _ for undisputed US *(27)* _ _ _ _ _ _ _ one, Howard. As of *(28)* _ _ _ _ _ 2010 (at South Africa 2010), Brad Guzan *(29)* _ _ _ earned ten caps *(30)* _ _ _ _ the US national *(31)* _ _ _ _ _ after putting in *(32)* _ _ _ _ _ service in the *(33)* _ _ _ _ _ _ set-up and starting *(34)* _ _ _ three of the *(35)* _ _ _ _ _ _ games at the *(36)* _ _ _ _ _ _ _ _ Football Tournament in *(37)* _ _ _ _ _ _ _ _ _ in the summer of 2008.

15

(Answer ID # 0493731)

1.	2.	3.
4.	5.	6.
7.	8.	9.
10.	11.	12.
13.	14.	15.
16.	17.	18.
19.	20.	21.
22.	23.	24.
25.	26.	27.
28.	29.	30.
31.	32.	33.
34.	35.	36.
37.		

Lesson 3
Marcus Hahnemann

Answer Key 0570273			
Word Bank			
Although	World	in	suffered
Bradley	a	international	the
CONCACAF	and	made	then
Cup	as	not	time
Hahnemann	called	of	to
Howard	career	on	various
Kasey	challenges	reflexes	veteran
Marcus	country	some	was
US	faith	spite	
USA	finals	squad	
United	friendly	sub	

Directions: Fill in each blank with a word from the word bank that best completes the story.

Hahnemann made his (1) _____ debut for the (2) _____ States national team (3) _____ November 19, 1994, in a 0–1 (4) _____ defeat to Trinidad (5) _____ Tobago. Marcus Hahnemann (6) _____ his first appearance (7) _____ a US jersey in 1994. (8) _____ Hahnemann played behind (9) _____ Keller and Tim (10) _____ as a goalkeeper in (11) _____ US national team. (12) _____ Marcus Hahnemann did (13) _____ see any playing (14) _____ in the 2010 FIFA (15) _____ Cup South Africa™, the (16) _____ showed in the (17) _____ by coach Bob (18) _____ was a testament (19) _____ the net-minder's strength (20) _____ character and quick (21) _____.

As a member of the 2010 World (22) _____ squad, Hahnemann had (23) _____ the misfortune of (24) _____ stiff competition for (25) _____ regular place in the (26) _____ team; behind at (27) _____ times in his (28) _____ were such standouts (29) _____ Keller, Brad Friedel and (30) _____ Tim Howard. In (31) _____ of all the (32) _____ he faced in the (33) _____ national team, Marcus (34) _____ proves impressive when (35) _____ upon by his (36) _____. Marcus Hahnemann was in the (37) _____ that won the (38) _____ Gold Cup in 1995 and (39) _____ also an unused (40) _____ in the FIFA World Cup (41) _____ in Germany in 2006.

Marcus Hahnemann (Answer ID # 0570273)

1.	2.	3.
4.	5.	6.
7.	8.	9.
10.	11.	12.
13.	14.	15.
16.	17.	18.
19.	20.	21.
22.	23.	24.
25.	26.	27.
28.	29.	30.
31.	32.	33.
34.	35.	36.
37.	38.	39.
40.	41.	

Answer Key 0419938
Word Bank

A-League	Rapids	at	on
After	Reading	college	same
As	Seattle	favorite	settling
Colorado	Sounders	former	signed
English	US	his	spells
Fulham	Wanderers	including	the
Hahnemann	Year	last	three
Hahnemann's	a	moved	two
Kasey	and	moving	when
Premier	appearances	named	with

Directions: Fill in each blank with a word from the word bank that best completes the story.

Marcus Hahnemann played *(1) GECLLOE* _____ soccer for the *(2) ETLTEAS* _____ Pacific University Falcons. *(3) EFTAR* _____ playing with distinction *(4) AT* _____ collegiate level in *(5) IHS* _____ native Washington – the *(6) AESM* _____ birth state as *(7) RREOMF* _____ USA goalkeeping great *(8) KSEYA* _____ Keller – Marcus Hahnemann *(9) SIEDNG* _____ up with the Seattle *(10) RSUOENDS* _____, where he spent *(11) TEHRE* _____ seasons in the *(12) US* _____ second tier before *(13) OGMNVI* _____ on to MLS *(14) DNA* _____ the Colorado Rapids.

(15) NSA'HENHMNA _____ professional career started *(16) HWEN* _____ he signed with *(17) EHT* _____ Seattle Sounders of the *(18) AGEEALU-* _____ on 1 May 1994. Marcus *(19) NAENMHHAN* _____ made 66 appearances in *(20) TOW* _____ seasons at the *(21) RAOOODLC* _____ Rapids) before moving *(22) ON* _____ to England, first *(23) IWTH* _____ Fulham on loan *(24) LPLSSE* _____ at Rochdale before *(25) LSGNITTE* _____ in at Reading.

(26) AS _____ a firm fan *(27) IEORFVTA* _____ at Reading, Marcus Hahnemann *(28) MDVEO* _____ on and spent the *(29) SALT* _____ season at Wolverhampton *(30) ERARWNDSE* _____ in England. At *(31) IDRAEGN* _____ Marcus Hahnemann made 276 *(32) NRPEESPCAAA* _____ for the club, *(33) ILNINCDUG* _____ spells in the *(34) RMEIERP* _____ League.

18. After two and *(35) A* _____ half seasons with the Colorado *(36) PADISR* _____ where he was *(37) ADNEM* _____ their Defender of the *(38) RYEA* _____, Marcus Hahnemann signed with *(39) LNSIGHE* _____ First Division club *(40) UHLMAF* _____, for £80,000 in June 1999.

(Answer ID # 0419938)

1.	2.	3.
4.	5.	6.
7.	8.	9.
10.	11.	12.
13.	14.	15.
16.	17.	18.
19.	20.	21.
22.	23.	24.
25.	26.	27.
28.	29.	30.
31.	32.	33.
34.	35.	36.
37.	38.	39.
40.		

Lesson 4
Jonathan Michael Paul Spector

Answer Key 1046333
Word Bank

Academy	States	club	made
After	U-17	coach	open
American	US	defense	played
Association	United	first	started
At	a	football	still
Chicago	already	graduated	sudden
Ferguson's	and	high	the
Finland	appearance	in	was
Jonathan	appearances	injuries	while
Manchester	as	joined	with
Spector	before	limited	youth
Spector's	being	lining	
St	career	loan	

Directions: Fill in each blank with a word from the word bank that best completes the story.

Jonathan Michael Paul *(1)* _____ is an American *(2)* _____ Football player who *(3)* _____ defense for the *(4)* _____ national soccer team *(5)* _____ English Premier League *(6)* _____ West Ham United. *(7)* _____ Spector made his *(8)* _____ USA senior national *(9)* _____ in 2003 against Jamaica.

Jonathan Spector *(10)* _____ from the United *(11)* _____ Soccer Federation's Bradenton *(12)* _____ in 2003. Jonathan Spector played *(13)* _____ school football at *(14)* _____. Viator High School and *(15)* _____ his club football *(16)* _____ with Schwaben AC *(17)* _____ Buffalo Grove, Illinois, *(18)* _____ joining national power *(19)* _____ Sockers. Jonathan Spector *(20)* _____ discovered by Manchester *(21)* _____ scout Jimmy Ryan *(22)* _____ playing for the *(23)* _____ Under-17 squad at *(24)* _____ Milk Cup in 2003.

Jonathan Spector *(25)* _____ up with world *(26)* _____ giants Manchester United in 2004 *(27)* _____ a teenager. At *(28)* _____ United Jonathan Spector *(29)* _____ a handful of *(30)* _____ for Sir Alex *(31)* _____ first team, before *(32)* _____ sent out on *(33)* _____ to Charlton Athletic in 2005.

Jonathan *(34)* _____ emergence in English football was *(35)* _____ and dramatic.

21

However *(36)* _____ blighted his rise and *(37)* _____ his playing time. *(38)* _____ an outstanding career *(39)* _____ the United States *(40)* _____ national team set-up, *(41)* _____ up at FIFA *(42)* _____ World Cup in *(43)* _____ in 2003, Jonathan Spector was *(44)* _____ chipping away at *(45)* _____ club career abroad. *(46)* _____ 24, Jonathan Spector was *(47)* _____ a useful option *(48)* _____ to USA head *(49)* _____, Bob Bradley in *(50)* _____ at South Africa 2010 FIFA World Cup though. Jonathan Spector has been partnered with captain Carlos Bocanegra in central defense occasionally due to Oguchi Onyewu's long-term injury.

Jonathan Michael Paul Spector

(Answer ID # 1046333)

1.	2.	3.
4.	5.	6.
7.	8.	9.
10.	11.	12.
13.	14.	15.
16.	17.	18.
19.	20.	21.
22.	23.	24.
25.	26.	27.
28.	29.	30.
31.	32.	33.
34.	35.	36.
37.	38.	39.

40.	41.	42.
43.	44.	45.
46.	47.	48.
49.	50.	

Answer Key 0830983
Word Bank

Africa	USA	for	right
Confederations	United	from	secured
Cup	World	him	shoulder
Cup™	a	in	side
FIFA	also	included	started
Gold	as	member	suffered
Hejduk	at	missed	take
Jonathan	back	moved	that
Netherlands	cement	national	the
Spector	could	of	to
States	entire	once	took
Steve	final	regained	where

Directions: Fill in each blank with a word from the word bank that best completes the story.

In 2006, Jonathan Spector *(1) EVMOD* _____ to West Ham *(2) IUEDTN* _____ in London, UK *(3) WREHE* _____ he has now *(4) ANERGIED* _____ his fitness and *(5) DEUSCRE* _____ regular first-team football *(6) EONC* _____ again. However injuries *(7) DREUSFEF* _____ before Spector's move *(8) FRMO* _____ Manchester United in *(9) EHT* _____ 2004-2005 season began to *(10) AETK* _____ a toll on *(11) MIH* _____ as he began *(12) TO* _____ gain a reputation *(13) AS* _____ injury-prone. Jonathan Spector *(14) ISMESD* _____ the 2005 lined up *(15) FRO* _____ the United States *(16) AT* _____ the FIFA U-20 *(17) LRWOD* _____ Cup in the *(18) NNDHELESRTA* _____ due to a *(19) OSDHULER* _____ injury. Jonathan Spector *(20) AOSL* _____ missed the 2006 FIFA World *(21) PC™U* _____ in Germany; he *(22) COUDL* _____ not be included *(23) IN* _____ then-coach Bruce Arena's *(24) EIDS* _____ as a result *(25) OF* _____ the shoulder injury.

(26) NTAANOJH _____ Spector was a *(27) RMEEMB* _____ of the team *(28) HATT* _____ won the 2007 CONCACAF *(29) OGLD* _____ Cup.

23

Following injuries to *(30) ESTVE* _____ Cherundolo and Frankie *(31) KDHEUJ* _____, Jonathan Spector was *(32) DIUCNDEL* _____ in the United *(33) TEASTS* _____ roster for the 2009 *(34) AFFI* _____ Confederations Cup and *(35) TKOO* _____ the chance to *(36) CNMETE* _____ his place in the *(37) NOLTAINA* _____ team, starting at *(38) GHRTI* _____ back for the *(39) TIERNE* _____ tournament. Jonathan Spector *(40) DSTREAT* _____ every game as the *(41) SUA* _____ surged to the *(42) ANFIL* _____ of the 2009 FIFA *(43) AESNCOFEOITDNR* _____ Cup in South *(44) AACIFR* _____. Having returned from *(45) A* _____ long injury lay-off, Jonathan *(46) PCERTOS* _____ was ever present at right *(47) BCAK* _____ for the remaining 2010 World *(48) PUC* _____ fourth round qualifers in 2009.

(Answer ID # 0830983)

1.	2.	3.
4.	5.	6.
7.	8.	9.
10.	11.	12.
13.	14.	15.
16.	17.	18.
19.	20.	21.
22.	23.	24.
25.	26.	27.
28.	29.	30.
31.	32.	33.
34.	35.	36.
37.	38.	39.

40.	41.	42.
43.	44.	45.
46.	47.	48.

Lesson 5
Carlos Manuel Bocanegra

Answer Key 0362410			
Word Bank			
Africa	Team	cause	player
Although	US	first-choice	primarily
Bocanegra	United	for	reprised
Carlos	a	friendly	seen
Cup	against	has	team
England	always	his	that
FIFA	and	in	the
Gold	as	is	then
June	at	line	time
Now	back	made	victory
Rennes	became	national	was
Spain	captaincy	of	
States	captained	played	

Directions: Fill in each blank with a word from the word bank that best completes the story.

Carlos Manuel Bocanegra *(1)* _ _ _ an American soccer *(2)* _ _ _ _ _ _ who also plays *(3)* _ _ _ French Ligue 1 club *(4)* _ _ _ _ _ _ _. Carlos Bocanegra captained *(5)* _ _ _ _ USA's to South *(6)* _ _ _ _ _ _ FIFA 2010 World Cup. *(7)* _ _ _ _ _ _ _ _ he is primarily *(8)* _ centre back, Carlos *(9)* _ _ _ _ _ _ _ _ _ has also seen *(10)* _ _ _ _ at left back *(11)* _ _ _ defensive midfielder. Carlos Bocanegra *(12)* _ _ an uncompromising centre-back, *(13)* _ _ _ _ _ _ willing to put *(14)* _ _ _ body on the *(15)* _ _ _ _ for the American *(16)* _ _ _ _ _. Although he is *(17)* _ _ _ _ _ _ _ _ _ _ a centre back, *(18)* _ _ _ _ _ _ Bocanegra has also *(19)* _ _ _ _ time at left *(20)* _ _ _ _ and defensive midfielder.

Carlos Bocanegra *(21)* _ _ _ _ _ _ the first-choice captain for *(22)* _ _ _ national team in 2008. Carlos Bocanegra *(23)* _ _ _ _ _ _ _ _ _ _ the US national *(24)* _ _ _ _ for the first time *(25)* _ _ a 4–1 U.S. *(26)* _ _ _ _ _ _ _ _ in a June 2, 2007, *(27)* _ _ _ _ _ _ _ _ against China and *(28)* _ _ _ _ _ _ _ _ _ the role throughout the 2007 *(29)* _ _ _ _ Cup. In 2008, Bocanegra was *(30)* _ _ _ _ _ _ _ _ _ _ _ _ captain for the *(31)* _ _ _ _ _ _ _ _ team. Carlos Bocanegra captained the *(32)* _ _ _ _ _ _ States national team *(33)* _ _ _ _ defeated No. 1 ranked *(34)* _ _ _ _ _ to win one *(35)* _ _ the 2009 FIFA Confederations *(36)* _ _ _ semi-final games on *(37)* _ _ _ _ 24, 2009.

Carlos Bocanegra continued his *(38)* _ _ _ _ _ _ _ _ _ duties throughout the 2010 *(39)* _ _ _ _ World Cup, starting *(40)* _ _ left back against *(41)* _ _ _ _ _ _ _ and Slovenia and *(42)* _ _ _ _ as the left-center back *(43)* _ _ _ _ _ _ _ Algeria and Ghana. *(44)* _ _ _ at 29, Carlos Bocanegra *(45)* _ _ _ _ his first appearance for the *(46)* _ _ national team back in 2001 and *(47)* _ _ _ _ amassed over 60 caps *(48)* _ _ of June 2010. Bocanegra *(49)* _ _ _ _ _ _ _ for the United *(50)* _ _ _ _ _ _ _ at the 1999 FIFA World Youth Championship and earned his first senior cap for the U.S. on December 9, 2001, against South Korea. Since 2007, when Carlos Bocanegra is available and in the US squad, he wears the captain's armband and always commands respect. As of July 2010 Carlos Bocanegra had scored 10 goals with his US squad, most with his head.

Carlos Manuel Bocanegra
(Answer ID # 0362410)

1.	2.	3.
4.	5.	6.
7.	8.	9.
10.	11.	12.
13.	14.	15.
16.	17.	18.
19.	20.	21.
22.	23.	24.
25.	26.	27.
28.	29.	30.
31.	32.	33.
34.	35.	36.
37.	38.	39.
40.	41.	42.

43.	44.	45.
46.	47.	48.
49.	50.	

Answer Key 0289769
Word Bank

Angeles	University	his	team
Bocanegra	a	in	that
Carlos	and	key	the
Chicago	born	made	to
Cup	champion)	new	top
Fire	defender	of	was
In	earned	player	with
MLS	fledgling	playing	year
Major	four	season	
Open	fourth	signed	
US	he	south	

Directions: Fill in each blank with a word from the word bank that best completes the story.

Carlos Bocanegra was *(1) ONBR* _____ in California, but *(2) HE* _____ has roots from *(3) TOSHU* _____ of the border *(4) IN* _____ Mexico. Carlos Bocanegra *(5) DGESNI* _____ a Project-40 contract *(6) TWHI* _____ Major League Soccer (MLS) *(7) NAD* _____ was drafted by *(8) TEH* _____ Chicago Fire with the *(9) UOFHRT* _____ overall pick in the 2000 *(10) LMS* _____ Super Draft after *(11) PYNIGLA* _____ college soccer at *(12) TIVRNIYUSE* _____ of California, Los *(13) SLEGEAN* _____ (UCLA).

Carlos Bocanegra made *(14) A* _____ name for himself in *(15) ORAMJ* _____ League Soccer with *(16) DIGLFLGEN* _____ Midwestern outfit Chicago *(17) REIF* _____. In his first *(18) SNSOAE* _____, in 2000, Carlos Bocanegra *(19) DMEA* _____ an impact in *(20) HSI* _____ Midwestern outfit Chicago *(21) AMET* _____ as the best *(22) ENW* _____ player in the *(23) US* _____ Major Soccer League (MSL). *(24) IN* _____ his first MSL season, in 2000, *(25) LOACRS* _____ Bocanegra was the *(26) KYE* _____ defender with his *(27) GCCIAHO* _____ team, and he *(28) ENRDAE* _____ the MSL's 'rookie of the *(29) YERA* _____,' handed out annually *(30) TO* _____ the best new *(31) LPYEAR* _____ in the US *(32) TPO* _____ flight in 2000. In his *(33) OFUR* _____ seasons with the Chicago Fire, Carlos *(34) ACNRGAEOB* _____ reached the MLS *(35) CPU* _____ final (the one-off game *(36) TTAH* _____ decides the MLS *(37) OANH)CMIP*

28

_____, won the US *(38) NEOP* _____ Cup (the American version *(39) OF* _____ England's FA Cup) and *(40) SAW* _____ twice named MLS *(41) DEEFDERN* _____ of the Year, in 2002 and 2003.

(Answer ID # 0289769)

1.	2.	3.
4.	5.	6.
7.	8.	9.
10.	11.	12.
13.	14.	15.
16.	17.	18.
19.	20.	21.
22.	23.	24.
25.	26.	27.
28.	29.	30.
31.	32.	33.
34.	35.	36.
37.	38.	39.
40.	41.	

Answer Key 0634739
Word Bank

Bocanegra	Wigan	even	saw
Bocanegra's	a	first	scorer
Carlos	all	he	snuff
Cottage	also	his	stint
Despite	among	holding	surplus
English	and	in	the
Fulham	back	left-back	to
League	bargain	midfield	twice
May	behind	new	was
McBride	branched	no-nonsense	win
Premier	came	of	with
September	captained	player	
While	embarked	released	

Directions: Fill in each blank with a word from the word bank that best completes the story.

Carlos Bocanegra was *(1)* _____ first player to *(2)* _____ the MLS Defender *(3)* _____ the Year Award *(4)* _____, in 2002 and 2003. Carlos *(5)* _____ rugged ability to *(6)* _____ out opposition attacks *(7)* _____ neutralize strikers led *(8)* _____ a move to *(9)* _____ Premier League outfit *(10)* _____ in 2004, where he *(11)* _____ on a successful *(12)* _____, playing 124 games and *(13)* _____ scoring 12 goals in the *(14)* _____. With Fulham, Carlos *(15)* _____ played primarily as *(16)* _____ centre back, but *(17)* _____ as a left *(18)* _____ and briefly as a *(19)* _____ midfielder. During the 2006–07 *(20)* _____ League season, Carlos Bocanegra *(21)* _____ Fulham's second leading *(22)* _____ with five goals, *(23)* _____ fellow American Brian *(24)* _____. On September 1, 2007, Carlos Bocanegra *(25)* _____ Fulham for the *(26)* _____ time in a Premier *(27)* _____ match where they *(28)* _____ from behind 3–3 draw *(29)* _____ Tottenham Hotspur.

On *(30)* _____ 15, 2007, Carlos Bocanegra made *(31)* _____ 100th appearance in the Premier League, *(32)* _____ for Fulham, against *(33)* _____ Athletic and was *(34)* _____ by Fulham on *(35)* _____ 23, 2008 to join Rennes *(36)* _____ France in June 2008. *(37)* _____ in England, Carlos Bocanegra *(38)* _____ out as a *(39)* _____, lining up as *(40)* _____ and occasionally in a holding *(41)* _____ role with Fulham. *(42)* _____ being a favorite *(43)* _____ fans at Craven *(44)* _____ for his dedication and *(45)* _____ play, the arrival of *(46)* _____ manger Roy Hodgson *(47)* _____ Carlos Bocanegra become *(48)* _____ to requirements and *(49)* _____ was released in May 2008. *(50)* _____ Bocanegra was signed by Stade Rennais in June 2008.

Since May 2008 when Bocanegra was released from Fulham, he has moved on to France's top flight with Rennes.

(Answer ID # 0634739)

1.	2.	3.
4.	5.	6.
7.	8.	9.
10.	11.	12.
13.	14.	15.
16.	17.	18.
19.	20.	21.
22.	23.	24.
25.	26.	27.
28.	29.	30.
31.	32.	33.
34.	35.	36.
37.	38.	39.
40.	41.	42.
43.	44.	45.
46.	47.	48.
49.	50.	

Lesson 6
Oguchialu Chijioke Onyewu

Answer Key 0945458
Word Bank

A	USA	defensive	performances
AC	United	final	player
CONCACAF	World	footballer	popularly
FIFA	a	gives	since
Germany	all	goalkeepers	size
Gold	as	gridiron	soccer
Milan	at	his	sports
Oguchi	back	in	the
Onyewu	been	kg	though
Panama	bite	mobile	to
S	combines	more	was
States	contract	of	
Tim	create	on	

Directions: Fill in each blank with a word from the word bank that best completes the story.

Oguchialu Chijioke Onyewu *(1)* _ _ _ _ _ _ _ _ _ _ known as "Oguchi" *(2)* _ _ _ _ _ _ _ is an American *(3)* _ _ _ _ _ _ player who played *(4)* _ _ a defender for *(5)* _ _ _ _ _ _ of Italy's Serie *(6)* _ and the United *(7)* _ _ _ _ _ _ national team. According *(8)* _ _ South Africa 2010 FIFA *(9)* _ _ _ _ _ _ _ report, Oguchi Onyewu "looks *(10)* _ _ _ _ like an American *(11)* _ _ _ _ _ _ _ _ player than a *(12)* _ _ _ _ _ _ _ _ _ _ but Oguchi Onyewu *(13)* _ _ _ _ _ Bob Bradley's USA *(14)* _ _ _ _ _, power and a *(15)* _ _ _ _ _ at the back." *(16)* _ _ _ _ _ _ _ Onyewu is 1.93m and 95 *(17)* _ _ but is surprisingly *(18)* _ _ _ _ _ _ _ and agile. As *(19)* _ _ South Africa 2010, Onyewu *(20)* _ _ _ the tallest outfield *(21)* _ _ _ _ _ _ _ ever in U.*(22)* _ _ team history; two *(23)* _ _ _ _ _ _ _ _ _ _ _ _ have been taller *(24)* _ _ _ _ _ _.

Oguchi Onyewu made *(25)* _ _ _ first appearance for *(26)* _ _ _ senior national team *(27)* _ _ October 13, 2004, against Panama. Oguchi Onyewu *(28)* _ _ _ _ _ _ _ _ _ well with central *(29)* _ _ _ _ _ _ _ _ _ _ partner Carlos Bocanegra to *(30)* _ _ _ _ _ _ _ a watertight seal *(31)* _ _ front of goalkeeper *(32)* _ _ _ Howard. For the *(33)* _ _ _ _ _ _ States, Onyewu has *(34)* _ _ _ _ _ a rock at the *(35)* _ _ _ _ _, neutralizing opposition strikers *(36)* _ _ _ _ _ _ his 2004 debut against *(37)* _ _ _ _ _ _ _ _. Oguchi Onyewu started *(38)* _ _ _ _ three games for the United States at the *(39)* _ _ _ _ _ World Cup™ in *(40)* _ _ _ _ _ _ _ _ in 2006 and was *(41)* _ crucial cog in the *(42)* _ _ _ _ _ _ _ _ _ _ Gold Cup-winning sides *(43)* _ _ 2005, 2007 and 2009. Oguchi Onyewu's *(44)* _ _ _ _ _ _ _ _ _ _ _ _ _ in the 2009 CONCACAF *(45)* _

_ _ _ Cup competition, where *(46)* _ _ _ went to the *(47)* _ _ _ _ _, earned Onyewu a *(48)* _ _ _ _ _ _ _ _ at Italian giants *(49)* _ _ Milan. In a *(50)* _ _ _ _ _ Cup qualifier draw against Costa Rica on October 14, 2009, Onyewu suffered a patellar tendon rupture.

Oguchi Onyewu played for the U.S. in the 2006 World Cup, and started in all three United States games. In the 2006 World Cup, Onyewu conceded a penalty from which Ghana scored, and the U.S. were eliminated with the resultant 2–1 defeat. Oguchi Onyewu has also represented the U.S. at various youth levels, including at the 2001 World Youth Championship.

Oguchialu Chijioke Onyewu
(Answer ID # 0945458)

1.	2.	3.
4.	5.	6.
7.	8.	9.
10.	11.	12.
13.	14.	15.
16.	17.	18.
19.	20.	21.
22.	23.	24.
25.	26.	27.
28.	29.	30.
31.	32.	33.
34.	35.	36.
37.	38.	39.
40.	41.	42.
43.	44.	45.

46.	47.	48.
49.	50.	

Answer Key 0443469
Word Bank

Andrew	Standard	eventually	parents
Belgian	States	for	played
Belgium	University	grew	program
Belgium's	Washington	have	quickly
France	and	he	shores
Liege	as	hit	team
Liège	attend	in	the
Maryland	before	landed	to
Metz	but	later	was
Oguchi	bypassed	moved	with
Onyewu	citizenship	of	years
Sherwood	college	only	
Spring	established	out	

Directions: Fill in each blank with a word from the word bank that best completes the story.

Oguchi Onyewu is *(1) OF* _____ Nigerian descent. Onyewu's *(2) RTPNASE* _____ are Nigerians who *(3) OVDEM* _____ to the United *(4) ESSTTA* _____ from Nigeria to *(5) NTAEDT* _____ Howard University in *(6) GTSNHONWIA* _____, D.C. Oguchi *(7) ENUOYW* _____ also holds Belgian *(8) NIZISCPITHE* _____. He speaks English *(9) DNA* _____ fluent French. Oguchi Onyewu *(10) EWRG* _____ up in Silver *(11) PNIRSG* _____ and later Olney, *(12) MAADYRNL* _____, and attended St. *(13) AENDRW* _____ Apostle School and *(14) EOHRWDOS* _____ High School. Onyewu *(15) AYDEPL* _____ two years of *(16) LECOGLE* _____ soccer at Clemson *(17) BRYTIUIS* _____

Oguchi Onyewu enrolled in *(18) TEH* _____ U.S. residency *(19) MGPRORA* _____ in Bradenton, Florida, *(20) FEREOB* _____ returning to Sherwood *(21) TO* _____ graduate. After two *(22) ERSYA* _____ of collegiate football, Onyewu *(23) PABSYESD* _____ Major League Soccer and *(24) TIH* _____ out for European *(25) EHSORS* _____ in 2002 signing with *(26) ZMET* _____ of Ligue 1 in *(27) ENRFAC* _____ and later to *(28) UEBMGIL* _____.

In 2002 Oguchi Onyewu *(29) LADDEN* _____ in France's Ligue 1 *(30) TWHI* _____ Metz, from where *(31) HE* _____ was loaned to *(32) IE'SGLBMU* _____ La Louvière. In 2003, *(33) ICHGUO* _____ Onyewu was loaned *(34) OTU* _____ to La Louvière *(35) IN* _____ Belgium, and to *(36) SATNADDR* _____ Liège a year *(37) EATLR* _____.

34

The move to *(38) IèLEG* _____ was made permanent *(39) OFR* _____ the 2004–05 season. In 2004 Oguchi Onyewu *(40) EVLLUYAENT* _____ made a home in Belgium and *(41) TSSHEBADEIL* _____ himself at Standard *(42) GEIEL* _____ where he would *(43) AEHV* _____ 139 appearances with the *(44) TAEM* _____. At Standard Liege he *(45) LCKYIUQ* _____ became renowned not *(46) YNLO* _____ for his size, *(47) UBT* _____ his contributions to the team in 2004. Oguchi Onyewu *(48) SAW* _____ named to the *(49) LBNGAEI* _____ league's Best XI *(50) AS* _____ well as Foreign Player of the Year for 2005. On December 26, 2006, Onyewu was voted U.S. Soccer Athlete of the Year. He was the first defender to earn the award since Alexi Lalas in 1995.

(Answer ID # 0443469)

1.	2.	3.
4.	5.	6.
7.	8.	9.
10.	11.	12.
13.	14.	15.
16.	17.	18.
19.	20.	21.
22.	23.	24.
25.	26.	27.
28.	29.	30.
31.	32.	33.
34.	35.	36.
37.	38.	39.
40.	41.	42.

43.	44.	45.
46.	47.	48.
49.	50.	

Answer Key 0548518
Word Bank

Champions	Standard	few	on
Costa	World	has	out
Cup	a	he	return
Division	after	helped	rupture
England	against	his	season
First	alongside	in	substitute
Geordie	an	knee	suffered
Germinal	and	loss	that
In	appearing	must	the
July	club	national	to
League	coming	nature	unable
Milan	contract	nicknamed	
Onyewu	domestic	of	

Directions: Fill in each blank with a word from the word bank that best completes the story.

Oguchi Onyewu made *(1)* _____ debut for Newcastle *(2)* _____ Fulham on February 3, 2007, *(3)* _____ a week later *(4)* _____ his home debut *(5)* _____ Titus Bramble, in *(6)* _____ 2–1 victory over Liverpool. *(7)* _____ 2007, Onyewu was loaned *(8)* _____ to Newcastle United *(9)* _____ the English Premier *(10)* _____, but he was *(11)* _____ to adapt to *(12)* _____ speed and frenetic *(13)* _____ of the game in *(14)* _____, returning to Liege *(15)* _____ only 11 appearances for the *(16)* _____ outfit.

Oguchi Onyewu *(17)* _____ Standard Liege to the 2007/2008 *(18)* _____ title upon his *(19)* _____ to Belgium. Oguchi *(20)* _____ made his 100th Belgian *(21)* _____ Division appearance for *(22)* _____ Liège on March 14, 2008, against *(23)* _____ Beerschot, and was *(24)* _____ integral part of the *(25)* _____ as they went *(26)* _____ a 29-match unbeaten streak *(27)* _____ win the 2007–08 Belgian First *(28)* _____

Oguchi Onyewu, also *(29)* _____ 'Gooch' signed a three-year *(30)* _____ with AC Milan on *(31)* _____ 7, 2009. Onyewu missed all the 2009–10 *(32)* _____ with AC

36

Milan – *(33)* _____ in only one *(34)* _____ League match – due a *(35)* _____ injury suffered while on *(36)* _____ team duty. It *(37)* _____ also be recalled *(38)* _____ in a World *(39)* _____ qualifier draw against *(40)* _____ Rica on October 14, 2009, Onyewu *(41)* _____ a patellar tendon *(42)* _____. Oguchi Onyewu made his *(43)* _____ debut on July 22, *(44)* _____ on as a *(45)* _____ for Alessandro Nesta in a *(46)* _____ to Club América in the *(47)* _____ Football Challenge. On a *(48)* _____ occasions Oguchi Onyewu *(49)* _____ been a victim *(50)* _____ racism; the most well-publicized incident occurred in the 2008–09 Championship playoff when Anderlecht defender Jelle Van Damme, according to Onyewu, repeatedly called him a "dirty ape," even after Onyewu relayed the information to the referees nothing was done about it. On June 2, 2009, shortly following the alleged racism remarks of Jelle Van Damme, it was announced by Onyewu's lawyer that he was suing Van Damme in an effort to end on-field racism in European soccer.

(Answer ID # 0548518)

1. _____	2. _____	3. _____
4. _____	5. _____	6. _____
7. _____	8. _____	9. _____
10. _____	11. _____	12. _____
13. _____	14. _____	15. _____
16. _____	17. _____	18. _____
19. _____	20. _____	21. _____
22. _____	23. _____	24. _____
25. _____	26. _____	27. _____
28. _____	29. _____	30. _____
31. _____	32. _____	33. _____
34. _____	35. _____	36. _____
37. _____	38. _____	39. _____

40. _____	41. _____	42. _____
43. _____	44. _____	45. _____
46. _____	47. _____	48. _____
49. _____	50. _____	

Lesson 7
Steven Cherundolo

Answer Key 0729452 Word Bank			
Arena	U	from	since
Armas	USA	has	strong
Bob	United	helps	struggling
Bundesliga	a	in	sustained
CONCACAF	an	injury	the
Cherundolo	and	missed	throughout
Cup	attended	national	to
FIFA	back	of	tournament
Hannover	defender	on	training
School	event	one	unable
States	favorite	position	who
Steve	first	prematurely	
Team	for	returned	

Directions: Fill in each blank with a word from the word bank that best completes the story.

Steven Cherundolo is *(1)* _ _ American soccer player, *(2)* _ _ _ _ played as a *(3)* _ _ _ _ _ _ _ _ _ for the United *(4)* _ _ _ _ _ _ _ national team and *(5)* _ _ _ _ _ _ _ _ _ _ 96 of the German *(6)* _ _ _ _ _ _ _ _ _ _.

Steve Cherundolo is *(7)* _ native of California who *(8)* _ _ _ _ _ to make a *(9)* _ _ _ _ _ _ _ rearguard for Team *(10)* _ _ _. He grew up *(11)* _ _ San Diego and *(12)* _ _ _ _ _ _ _ _ _ Mt. Carmel High *(13)* _ _ _ _ _ _ _ in Rancho Penasquitos. *(14)* _ _ _ _ _ Cherundolo earned his *(15)* _ _ _ _ _ cap for the *(16)* _ _ _ _ _ _ States national team *(17)* _ _ _ _ _ in 1999 and has *(18)* _ _ _ _ _ _ been a sturdy *(19)* _ _ _ _ reliable right-back for *(20)* _ _ _ _ _ USA in spite *(21)* _ _ injuries. Cherundolo was *(22)* _ _ Team USA roster *(23)* _ _ _ _ the 2002 FIFA World *(24)* _ _ _ after a late *(25)* _ _ _ _ _ _ _ replacement for Chris *(26)* _ _ _ _ _ _. All the same, *(27)* _ _ _ _ _ _ _ _ _ _ himself was injured in *(28)* _ _ _ _ _ _ _ _ _ _ shortly before the *(29)* _ _ _ _ _ _ began and was *(30)* _ _ _ _ _ _ _ to play.

In *(31)* _ _ _ 2005 CONCACAF Gold Cup, Cherundolo *(32)* _ _ _ _ _ _ _ _ _ _ _ a knee injury *(33)* _ _ _ _ _ a tackle that *(34)* _ _ _ _ _ _ _ _ _ _ _ _ _ _ ended his participation in the *(35)* _ _ _ _ _ _ _ _ _ _ _ _. Steve also Cherundolo *(36)* _ _ _ _ _ _ _ out on the 2009 *(37)* _ _ _ _ Confederations Cup due *(38)* _ _ another injury but *(39)* _ _ _ _ _ _ _ _ _ to captain the *(40)* _.S. during the 2009 *(41)* _ _ _ _ _ _ _ _ _ _ Gold Cup. Despite *(42)* _ _ _ _ _ _ _ _ _ _ with serious injuries *(43)* _ _ _ _ _ _ _ _ _ _ _ his career with United States *(44)* _ _ _ _ _ _ _ _ _ team, Steve Cherundolo *(45)* _ _ _ _ established himself as a *(46)* _ _ _ _ _ _ _ _

_ in his chosen *(47)* _ _ _ _ _ _ _ _, first for Bruce *(48)* _ _ _ _ _ and then for *(49)* _ _ _ Bradley. Steve Cherundolo was *(50)* _ _ _ of seven defenders named to the Team USA squad for the 2010 World Cup in South Africa. Steve Cherundolo was a member of the 2005 CONCACAF Gold Cup winning side, but missed out on USA's run to the final of the 2009 FIFA Confederations Cup through injury. By South Africa 2010 FIFA World Cup tournament, Steve Cherundolo had amassed 57 caps for the USA and scored two goals. Steve Cherundolo started all four of the 2010 World Cup in South Africa games at right back for the USA during their run to the final 16.

Steven Cherundolo
(Answer ID # 0729452)

1.	2.	3.
4.	5.	6.
7.	8.	9.
10.	11.	12.
13.	14.	15.
16.	17.	18.
19.	20.	21.
22.	23.	24.
25.	26.	27.
28.	29.	30.
31.	32.	33.
34.	35.	36.
37.	38.	39.
40.	41.	42.

43.	44.	45.
46.	47.	48.
49.	50.	

Answer Key 0388701
Word Bank

American	a	desire	roster
Before	and	for	season
California	as	has	story
Cherundolo	bee	helped	summers
Germany	before	in	team
Hannover	captain's	into	the
La	college	of	times
Premier	contract	played	to
Steve	country's	positional	top
University	decade	remain	under
Wanderers	declined	right-back	years

Directions: Fill in each blank with a word from the word bank that best completes the story.

With only two (1) *RESAY* _____ of University football (2) *UDNER* _____ his belt, Steve (3) *NCHRUOEDOL* _____ moved to Germany (4) *IN* _____ 1999, lining up with (5) *NROAHVEN* _____ 96 who were then in (6) *TEH* _____ second division of the (7) *NR'CTOYUS* _____ professional set-up. In the 2001/2002 (8) *OAESSN* _____, after establishing himself (9) *AS* _____ first-choice in the (10) *ARBKHGC-TI* _____ position, Steve Cherundolo (11) *PLHEDE* _____ his Hannover 96 side (12) *TO* _____ a spot in the (13) *OTP* _____ flight, where they (14) *NMEIAR* _____ to this day (15) *OF* _____ June 2010. In 2005, English (16) *IRREPEM* _____ League side Bolton (17) *RESWRAEDN* _____ F.C. agreed to (18) *A* _____ deal with Hannover (19) *ROF* _____ Cherundolo, but he (20) *NEDECDIL* _____, opting to remain in (21) *RGAENMY* _____. Steve Cherundolo signed (22) *OCATRNTC* _____ extensions with Hannover in the (23) *UMRESMS* _____ of 2007 and 2010.

Steve Cherundolo (24) *AHS* _____ occasionally donned the (25) *SITA'NACP* _____ armband for Hannover 96. (26) *ERFEBO* _____ joining Hannover 96, Cherundolo (27) *LDYEPA* _____ two years of (28) *LLCGEEO* _____ soccer at the (29) *UVRYNETIIS* _____ of Portland, from 1997 to 1998. (30) *SEVTE* _____ Cherundolo played for the (31) *LA* _____ Jolla Nomads club (32) *MATE* _____ which won the (33) *IAILNFORAC* _____ State Championship six (34) *ITMES* _____ with him on the (35)

41

TSRREO _____ as a youth *(36) FERBEO* _____ entering. Strong, dependable *(37) NAD* _____ with a sharp *(38) PTLNIOSOAI* _____ sense Steve Cherundolo has the *(39) ESEIDR* _____ to get up *(40) NTOI* _____ attack. As an *(41) EAINCRAM* _____ Youth soccer star, Steve Cherundolo has *(42) EEB* _____ an American success *(43) RSOYT* _____ overseas for a *(44) EDDACE* _____ now.

(Answer ID # 0388701)

1.	2.	3.
4.	5.	6.
7.	8.	9.
10.	11.	12.
13.	14.	15.
16.	17.	18.
19.	20.	21.
22.	23.	24.
25.	26.	27.
28.	29.	30.
31.	32.	33.
34.	35.	36.
37.	38.	39.
40.	41.	42.
43.	44.	

Lesson 8
Jonathan Bornstein

Answer Key 0903185 Word Bank			
Africa	United	game	player
Bob	against	he	round
Bornstein	an	his	sitting
Bradley	and	in	solid
Cup	club	new	started
Jonathan	difficult	of	substitute
South	final	one	the
US	found	option	two

Directions: Fill in each blank with a word from the word bank that best completes the story.

Jonathan Bornstein was *(1)* _ _ _ of the relatively *(2)* _ _ _ members of the *(3)* _ _ national squad at *(4)* _ _ _ _ _ Africa 2010 FIFA World *(5)* _ _ _. Jonathan Bornstein soon *(6)* _ _ _ _ _ his way into *(7)* _ _ _ Bradley's reckoning after *(8)* _ _ _ _ _ performances with MLS *(9)* _ _ _ _ side Chivas USA *(10)* _ _ 2007. At South Africa 2010, *(11)* _ _ _ _ _ _ _ _ Bornstein found it *(12)* _ _ _ _ _ _ _ _ _ to hold to *(13)* _ _ _ _ national team spot in *(14)* _ _ _ left-back position but *(15)* _ _ represented a versatile *(16)* _ _ _ _ _ _ _ to coach Bob *(17)* _ _ _ _ _ _ _ _ _, especially during times *(18)* _ _ injury crisis. Jonathan *(19)* _ _ _ _ _ _ _ _ _ _ is the kind of *(20)* _ _ _ _ _ _ _ who could make *(21)* _ _ impact on a *(22)* _ _ _ _ _ even as a *(23)* _ _ _ _ _ _ _ _ _ _ _. In the South *(24)* _ _ _ _ _ _ _ 2010 FIFA World Cup Jonathan Bornstein *(25)* _ _ _ _ _ _ _ _ at left back *(26)* _ _ _ _ _ _ _ _ Algeria in the *(27)* _ _ _ _ _ _ group play game *(28)* _ _ _ against Ghana in the *(29)* _ _ _ _ _ of sixteen after *(30)* _ _ _ _ _ _ _ _ out the first *(31)* _ _ _ _ group-stage games for the *(32)* _ _ _ _ _ _ _ States.

Jonathan Bornstein
(Answer ID # 0903185)

1.	2.	3.
4.	5.	6.
7.	8.	9.

10.	11.	12.
13.	14.	15.
16.	17.	18.
19.	20.	21.
22.	23.	24.
25.	26.	27.
28.	29.	30.
31.	32.	

Answer Key 0585964
Word Bank

Bornstein	also	got	preferred
Cal	and	had	relegated
Confederations	assist	in	since
In	attacking	joining	spring
Jewish	back	knee	started
Jonathan	bounced	left-back	team
Los	career	lost	the
Mexican	caused	matches	to
U	college	midfield	where
UCLA	crisis	of	with
US	due	on	years
a	first	played	
against	for	players	

Directions: Fill in each blank with a word from the word bank that best completes the story.

Jonathan Bornstein is *(1) OF* _____ mixed Mexican and *(2) HJSWEI* _____ heritage. He is Jewish *(3) ON* _____ his father's side *(4) DNA* _____ his mother is *(5) ENIAMXC* _____. Jonathan Bornstein attended *(6) OLS* _____ Alamitos High School *(7)*

44

HWEER _____ he played soccer *(8) FRO* _____ all four years. *(9) JTAHNANO* _____ Bornstein started his *(10) ELCGOEL* _____ soccer career at *(11) ACL* _____ Poly Pomona and *(12) PEYLAD* _____ there for two *(13) SRYEA* _____ before transferring to *(14) CULA* _____ for the 2004 season. Jonathan *(15) RINSNOTBE* _____ began his MLS *(16) CRAERE* _____ in 2007 playing either *(17) A* _____ striker or an *(18) TANCGAITK* _____ midfielder. He has *(19) OLSA* _____ played as a *(20) KLEAT-CBF* _____ for Bob Bradley *(21) UDE* _____ to a dearth of *(22) PESLYRA* _____ in that position *(23) SDAUCE* _____ by an injury *(24) IISCRS* _____. Coach Bradley, however, *(25) EEFRDREPR* _____ to use Bornstein *(26) IN* _____ the left-back position for *(27) HTE* _____ national team. Since *(28) JINNOIG* _____ the US National *(29) EMTA* _____ in 2007, Bornstein has *(30) CDEBNOU* _____ around the pitch *(31) WTIH* _____ appearances in attack, in *(32) IMIFDDEL* _____ and at the *(33) CABK* _____.

On January 20, 2007 Jonathan Bornstein *(34) TOG* _____ his first cap, and *(35) ITRFS* _____ goal on an *(36) ISTASS* _____ from Justin Mapp, for the *(37) U* _____.S. national team *(38) AGATSIN* _____ Denmark. By July 2010 Jonathan Bornstein *(39) AHD* _____ earned nearly 30 caps *(40) INCSE* _____ making his debut with the *(41) US* _____ national team in 2007. *(42) IN* _____ 2008, Jonathan Bornstein suffered a *(43) EKNE* _____ injury throughout the *(44) IRNGSP* _____. Struggling with injuries in 2008, Jonathan Bornstein *(45) TOSL* _____ his starting place *(46) TO* _____ Heath Pearce. Jonathan Bornstein *(47) ETSRTAD* _____ the group stage *(48) ECHATMS* _____ at the 2009 FIFA *(49) TCFRNANIOSOEDE* _____ Cup but was *(50) ATGEELDRE* _____ back to the bench when Carlos Bocanegra returned from injury. Jonathan Bornstein scored the equalizing goal in the United States' final World Cup qualifier against Costa Rica in the fifth minute of injury time.

(Answer ID # 0585964)

1.	2.	3.
4.	5.	6.
7.	8.	9.
10.	11.	12.
13.	14.	15.
16.	17.	18.
19.	20.	21.

22.	23.	24.
25.	26.	27.
28.	29.	30.
31.	32.	33.
34.	35.	36.
37.	38.	39.
40.	41.	42.
43.	44.	45.
46.	47.	48.
49.	50.	

Lesson 9
Jay Michael DeMerit

Answer Key 0788594 Word Bank			
C	Watford	headed	seek
Championship	Wisconsin	impressed	side
Chicago	a	in	signed
DeMerit	and	is	some
Development	briefly	joined	team
Following	college	matches	the
July	course	one	tier
League	defender	play-off	to
Port	earn	player	trial
Premier	for	playing	was
Ray	game's	pocket	with
United	graduated	season	
University	graduation	second	

Directions: Fill in each blank with a word from the word bank that best completes the story.

Jay Michael DeMerit *(1)* _____ an American soccer *(2)* _____ who played for *(3)* _____ States national soccer *(4)* _____ at South Africa 2010 *(5)* _____ captained Watford F.*(6)* _____. at one point *(7)* _____ time.

Born in *(8)* _____ frost-covered American north in *(9)* _____, DeMerit attended Bay *(10)* _____ High School and *(11)* _____ in 1998. He played *(12)* _____ soccer at the *(13)* _____ of Illinois at *(14)* _____ as forward and *(15)* _____. Jay DeMerit played *(16)* _____ for Chicago Fire *(17)* _____, the USL Premier *(18)* _____ League. As he *(19)* _____ not drafted or *(20)* _____ by any Major *(21)* _____ Soccer clubs following *(22)* _____ from college he *(23)* _____ to Europe to *(24)* _____ his fortune. Jay *(25)* _____ arrived in England in 2003 *(26)* _____ only $1,800 in his *(27)* _____ and started off *(28)* _____ in the ninth *(29)* _____ of English football *(30)* _____ Southall, earning only £40 *(31)* _____ week.

In July 2004, DeMerit *(32)* _____ Northwood, a seventh-tier *(33)* _____, to play in

47

(34) _____ of their pre-season *(35)* _____. Northwood played Championship side *(36)* _____, then a League *(37)* _____ side in their *(38)* _____ pre-season match. During the *(39)* _____ of the match, DeMerit *(40)* _____ then Watford manager *(41)* _____ Lewington enough to *(42)* _____ a two-week trial. *(43)* _____ his two week *(44)* _____ at Northwood in *(45)* _____ 2004, DeMerit signed a *(46)* _____ year contract with Watford *(47)* _____ play in their 2004–05 *(48)* _____.

On May 21, 2006, in the *(49)* _____ final against Leeds United, DeMerit headed in the *(50)* _____ first goal for Watford and was named Man of the Match as Watford gained promotion to the Premier League by defeating Leeds United 3-0.

Jay Michael DeMerit
(Answer ID # 0788594)

1.	2.	3.
4.	5.	6.
7.	8.	9.
10.	11.	12.
13.	14.	15.
16.	17.	18.
19.	20.	21.
22.	23.	24.
25.	26.	27.
28.	29.	30.
31.	32.	33.
34.	35.	36.
37.	38.	39.

40.	41.	42.
43.	44.	45.
46.	47.	48.
49.	50.	

Directions: Fill in each blank with a word from the word bank that best completes the story.

On May 21, 2006, in *(1)* _ _ _ play-off final against *(2)* _ _ _ _ _ _ United, DeMerit headed *(3)* _ _ the game's first *(4)* _ _ _ _ _ for Watford and *(5)* _ _ _ named Man of the *(6)* _ _ _ _ _ as Watford gained *(7)* _ _ _ _ _ _ _ _ _ to the Premier *(8)* _ _ _ _ _ _ by defeating Leeds *(9)* _ _ _ _ _ _ _ 3-0. DeMerit has since *(10)* _ _ _ _ a regular in the *(11)* _ _ _ _ _ _ _ lineup until 2010, when *(12)* _ _ was released from *(13)* _ _ _ contract. After nearly 170 *(14)* _ _ _ _ _ _ _ _ _ _ at Watford, DeMerit *(15)* _ _ _ _ _ _ _ the right to *(16)* _ _ _ _ Watford F.C's *(17)* _ _ _ _ _ _ _ _ on a few *(18)* _ Jay DeMerit's increased *(19)* _ _ _ _ _ _ overseas caught the *(20)* _ _ _ and attention of the *(21)* _ _ Soccer authority set-up in 2007. *(22)* _ _ was called in *(23)* _ _ the national team. *(24)* _ _ _ _ _ _ _ _ earned his first *(25)* _ _ _ _ cap, in March 2007, in *(26)* _ friendly against Guatemala. *(27)* _ _ _ DeMerit started with the US *(28)* _ _ _ _ _ _ _ _ team at the *(29)* _ _ _ _ _ _ _ _ _ _ USA campaign at the 2007 *(30)* _ _ _ _ _ _ _ _ Gold Cup putting in a *(31)* _ _ _ _ turn in defense *(32)* _ _ _ _ the US reached the *(33)* _ _ _ _ _ of the 2009 Confederations *(34)* _ _ _.

(Answer ID # 0390874)

1.	2.	3.
4.	5.	6.
7.	8.	9.
10.	11.	12.
13.	14.	15.
16.	17.	18.
19.	20.	21.
22.	23.	24.
25.	26.	27.
28.	29.	30.
31.	32.	33.
34.		

Lesson 10
Clarence Goodson

Answer Key 0794776
Word Bank

Dallas	abroad	established	scored
Gold	against	experimental	seasons
Goodson	also	go	soil
High	an	goal	success
IK	and	grab	the
In	as	his	to
June	at	in	top
Norwegian	called	leaping	was
Start	club	loss	who
States	coach	made	with
Virginia	college	moving	years
Woodson	contract	on	
a	defender	playing	

Directions: Fill in each blank with a word from the word bank that best completes the story.

Clarence Goodson is *(1)* _ _ American soccer player *(2)* _ _ _ played for United *(3)* _ _ _ _ _ _ _ national soccer team *(4)* _ _ South Africa 2010 and *(5)* _ _ _ _ played as a *(6)* _ _ _ _ _ _ _ _ _ _ _ for IK Start *(7)* _ _ Norway.

Clarence Goodson *(8)* _ _ _ _ born in Alexandria, *(9)* _ _ _ _ _ _ _ _ _ _ and attended Annandale *(10)* _ _ _ _ _ School his freshman *(11)* _ _ _ _ sophomore seasons before *(12)* _ _ _ _ _ _ _ to W.T. *(13)* _ _ _ _ _ _ _ _ _ High School. Clarence *(14)* _ _ _ _ _ _ _ _ _ began his professional *(15)* _ _ _ _ _ _ _ _ _ career with FC *(16)* _ _ _ _ _ _ _ in 2004 after three *(17)* _ _ _ _ _ _ of successfully playing at *(18)* _ _ _ _ _ _ _ _ _ level. In four *(19)* _ _ _ _ _ _ _ with his Texas *(20)* _ _ _ _, FC Dallas Clarence Goodson *(21)* _ _ _ _ _ 76 appearances and his *(22)* _ _ _ _ _ _ _ _ _ ability saw him *(23)* _ _ _ _ _ the odd goal *(24)* _ _ well on set-pieces. *(25)* _ _ 2008 Clarence Goodson decided *(26)* _ _ seek his fortune *(27)* _ _ _ _ _ _ _ and signed a *(28)* _ _ _ _ _ _ _ _ _ with Norwegian club *(29)* _ _ Start. He soon *(30)* _ _ _ _ _ _ _ _ _ _ _ _ _ himself as a *(31)* _ _ _ _ defender in the *(32)* _ _ _ _ _ _ _ _ _ _ _ _ league. As of *(33)* _ _ _ _ 2010, Clarence Goodson, had *(34)* _ _ _ _ _ _ _ 11 goals in 52 appearances *(35)* _ _ _ _ _ his Norwegian club, IK *(36)* _ _ _ _ _ _. Clarence Goodson made *(37)* _ _ _ international debit in *(38)* __ friendly against Sweden *(39)* __ __ January 19, 2008.

      Clarence Goodson's *(40)* _ _ _ _ _ _ overseas did not *(41)* _ _ unnoticed by USA *(42)* _ _ _ _ _ Bradley. Bob Bradley *(43)* _ _ _ _ _ _ Goodson into his *(44)* _ _ _ _ _ _ _ _ _ _ _ squad for 2009 CONCACAF *(45)* _ _ _ _ Cup on home *(46)* _ _ _ _, where he managed to grab a *(47)* _ _ _ _ in the semi-final *(48)* _ _ _ _ _ _ _ Honduras before a 5-0 *(49)* _ _ _ _ to Mexico in *(50)* _ _ _ final in New York.

As a big, tall and strong central defender with the US national team, Clarence Goodson was well needed by USA coach Bob Bradley with normal starter Oguchi Onyewu still recovering from a knee injury on the eve of the 2010 FIFA World Cup South Africa™.

Clarence Goodson
(Answer ID # 0794776)

1.	2.	3.
4.	5.	6.
7.	8.	9.
10.	11.	12.
13.	14.	15.
16.	17.	18.
19.	20.	21.
22.	23.	24.
25.	26.	27.
28.	29.	30.
31.	32.	33.
34.	35.	36.
37.	38.	39.

40.	41.	42.
43.	44.	45.
46.	47.	48.
49.	50.	

Lesson 11
Michael Bradley

Answer Key 0597953
Word Bank

Bradley	South	grew	son
Bulls	States	head	spent
Cup	a	headed	teenage
Fire	also	his	the
Illinois	ambitious	in	then
Major	among	join	to
MetroStars	an	just	transferred
Michael	and	local	was
Netherlands	at	midfielder	who
Princeton	broke	of	with
Red	coached	on	youngest
Soccer	father	professionals	
Sockers	force	serious	

Directions: Fill in each blank with a word from the word bank that best completes the story.

Michael Bradley is *(1)* _____ American soccer player *(2)* _____ played for United *(3)* _____ national soccer team *(4)* _____ South Africa 2010 and *(5)* _____ played as a *(6)* _____ for Borussia Mönchengladbach *(7)* _____ the German Fußball-Bundesliga. *(8)* _____ Bradley is the *(9)* _____ of US coach *(10)* _____, the US coach at *(11)* _____ Africa 2010 FIFA World *(12)* _____. Michael Bradley was raised *(13)* _____ football, first in *(14)* _____, New Jersey where *(15)* _____ father was the *(16)* _____ coach of the *(17)* _____ University team. He *(18)* _____ time watching from *(19)* _____ sidelines as his *(20)* _____ coached the Chicago *(21)* _____ of Major League *(22)* _____. Michael Bradley spent his *(23)* _____ years in Palatine, *(24)* _____ where his dad *(25)* _____ the Chicago Fire of *(26)* _____ League Soccer. He *(27)* _____ up playing for *(28)* _____ FC, who went *(29)* _____ the 2002 National Championship *(30)* _____ finished 3rd. In 2004, at *(31)* _____ 16 years of age, Michael Bradley *(32)* _____ signed by the *(33)* _____ (now the New York *(34)* _____ Bulls), who were *(35)* _____ coached by his father.

After *(36)* _____ slow start and a *(37)* _____ foot injury, even at 16 Michael Bradley *(38)* _____ into the team *(39)* _____ his second season *(40)* _____ the New York Red *(41)* _____ and proved a *(42)* _____ to be reckoned with *(43)* _____ far more experienced *(44)* _____.

In January 2006, Michael Bradley was *(45)* _____ to SC Heerenveen of *(46)* _____. The eager and *(47)* _____ young player, Michael Bradley, *(48)* _____ to Netherlands to *(49)* _____ Heerenveen and became the *(50)* _____ player to be sold by Major League Soccer.

Michael Bradley
(Answer ID # 0597953)

1.	2.	3.
4.	5.	6.
7.	8.	9.
10.	11.	12.
13.	14.	15.
16.	17.	18.
19.	20.	21.
22.	23.	24.
25.	26.	27.
28.	29.	30.
31.	32.	33.
34.	35.	36.
37.	38.	39.
40.	41.	42.
43.	44.	45.

46.	47.	48.
49.	50.	

Answer Key 0973909
Word Bank

Bayern	Mönchengladbach	eighty-first	move
Bradley	November	footballing	of
Bradley's	SC	game	proved
Dutch	The	glitz	season
German	be	headed	the
Holland	by	his	young
League	club's	join	
Monchengladbach	day	just	

Directions: Fill in each blank with a word from the word bank that best completes the story.

In January 2006, Michael *(1) EADLBRY* _____ was transferred to *(2) SC* _____ Heerenveen of Netherlands. *(3) TEH* _____ eager and ambitious *(4) YGNOU* _____ player, Michael Bradley, *(5) DHDEAE* _____ to Netherlands to *(6) JION* _____ Heerenveen and became *(7) TEH* _____ youngest player to *(8) BE* _____ sold by Major *(9) EGLAEU* _____ Soccer. While in the *(10) TCHUD* _____ top flight Michael Bradley *(11) DREVPO* _____ himself more than *(12) SJTU* _____ a midfield bruiser *(13) BY* _____ scoring 16 goals in the 2007-2008 *(14) EOASSN* _____ to become the *(15) SULBC'* _____ top marksman. Michael *(16) R'YEBDLSA* _____ impressive performance in *(17) AHNLDOL* _____ led to another *(18) EOVM* _____ at the beginning *(19) OF* _____ the 2008-2009 Season. On *(20) RBEVEOMN* _____ 15, 2008, Michael Bradley scored *(21) IHS* _____ first goal for *(22) MöNHAHGELNDCCBA* _____ against Bundesliga powerhouse *(23) NRBAYE* _____ Munich with an *(24) RIY-FGTHETSI* _____ minute equalizing header. The *(25) AEGM* _____ ended 2–2. He joined the *(26) IGLZT* _____ and glamour of the *(27) NEAMGR* _____ Bundesliga and Borussia *(28) OCCHLADGMEAHNNB* _____, where his club *(29) FOLOLAGNITB* _____ continues to this *(30) ADY* _____, July 25, 2010.

Michael Bradley
(Answer ID # 0973909)

1.	2.	3.
4.	5.	6.
7.	8.	9.
10.	11.	12.
13.	14.	15.
16.	17.	18.
19.	20.	21.
22.	23.	24.
25.	26.	27.
28.	29.	30.

Answer Key 0867346
Word Bank

Bradley	after	his	semifinal
CONCACAF	against	in	senior
Canada	as	international	sent
Cary	brought	late	start
Cup	challenge	match	substitute
FIFA	did	maturity	the
Michael	earned	not	then
S	following	of	to

States	fourth	off	train
U-20	game-winner	program	was
United	goal	putting	with
Uruguay	he	scored	second
a	helped	second	

Directions: Fill in each blank with a word from the word bank that best completes the story.

Michael Bradley earned *(1) SIH* _____ first international cap *(2) IN* _____ the May 26, 2006 match *(3) ITSNAAG* _____ Venezuela as a *(4) TTTSUIEBSU* _____. He again played his *(5) SONCED* _____ cap for the *(6) TNEUDI* _____ States in the *(7) OLWONILFG* _____ game against Latvia, *(8) AS* _____ a substitute. Although *(9) ONT* _____ yet a member *(10) OF* _____ the US squad *(11) THNE* _____, Michael Bradley was *(12) RUHTBOG* _____ into the 2006 World *(13) CPU* _____ training camp in *(14) YCAR* _____, North Carolina to *(15) AIRTN* _____ with the United *(16) ESASTT* _____ national team.

After *(17) ITPUTNG* _____ in his time *(18) TWHI* _____ the U-17 residency *(19) RPMORAG* _____ in Florida, Michael *(20) LRYBADE* _____ turned out for *(21) EHT* _____ USA at the *(22) AFIF* _____ U-20 World Cup in *(23) ACDANA* _____ in 2007, only days *(24) RFTEA* _____ helping the United States *(25) SNRIEO* _____ team to their *(26) ORHFTU* _____ CONCACAF Gold Cup. *(27) EAICMHL* _____ Bradley started every *(28) THCMA* _____ for the U.*(29) S* _____. at the 2007 FIFA *(30) -U20* _____ World Cup, where *(31) HE* _____ scored the game-winning *(32) LOAG* _____ in the 107th minute against *(33) RYUUAUG* _____ in the round of 16.

Michael Bradley *(34) RADNEE* _____ his first international *(35) TTASR* _____ on March 28, 2007, during *(36) A* _____ friendly against Guatemala. Michael Bradley *(37) WSA* _____ a starter at the 2007 *(38) AACNCFOC* _____ Gold Cup and *(39) HDPELE* _____ lead the U.S. *(40) TO* _____ the title, though he was *(41) TNSE* _____ off for a *(42) AELT* _____ tackle in the *(43) LIMESIAFN* _____ against Canada. Michael *(44) IDD* _____ show his lack of *(45) URYITMTA* _____ when he was sent *(46) FFO* _____ for a rash *(47) ECLNALEGH* _____ in the semi-final with Canada in 2007. Michael Bradley *(48) DSRECO* _____ his first senior *(49) AIIOTNRLENANT* _____ goal on October 17, 2007, with a *(50) REA-GNIWNME* _____ in the 87th minute against Switzerland in a friendly. Following these performances, Bradley was named U.S. Soccer's Young Athlete of the Year for 2007. Bradley has since become an indispensable member of the USA national team where his dad is now the coach (as of July 25, 2010).

(Answer ID # 0867346)

1.	2.	3.
4.	5.	6.
7.	8.	9.
10.	11.	12.
13.	14.	15.
16.	17.	18.
19.	20.	21.
22.	23.	24.
25.	26.	27.
28.	29.	30.
31.	32.	33.
34.	35.	36.
37.	38.	39.
40.	41.	42.
43.	44.	45.
46.	47.	48.
49.	50.	

Answer Key 0842035
Word Bank

Africa	Olympic	by	qualification
As	South	critical	side
Beijing	States	did	substitute
Bob	US	first	surged
Cup	USA	first-ever	the
FIFA	United	group	up
Football	World	his	was
Gold	a	in	where
Guatemala	against	instrumental	
March	an	key	
Michael	become	part	

Directions: Fill in each blank with a word from the word bank that best completes the story.

Michael Bradley earned *(1)* _ _ _ first international cap *(2)* _ _ the May 26, 2006 match *(3)* _ _ _ _ _ _ _ Venezuela as a *(4)* _ _ _ _ _ _ _ _ _ _ _. Michael Bradley earned his *(5)* _ _ _ _ _ international start on *(6)* _ _ _ _ _ 28, 2007, during a friendly against *(7)* _ _ _ _ _ _ _ _.

Michael Bradley is now *(8)* _ constant player in *(9)* _ _ _ US midfield, playing a *(10)* _ _ _ _ _ _ _ _ _ role in the 2007 *(11)* _ _ _ _ _ Cup campaign. He *(12)* _ _ _ _ in the lined *(13)* _ _ for the United *(14)* _ _ _ _ _ _ _ at the 2008 Olympic *(15)* _ _ _ _ _ _ _ _ _ Tournament in Beijing, *(16)* _ _ _ _ _ _ the US unfortunately *(17)* _ _ _ _ not advance beyond the *(18)* _ _ _ _ _ stage. Since the 2008 *(19)* _ _ _ _ _ _ _ _ Football Tournament in *(20)* _ _ _ _ _ _ _ _, Michael Bradley has *(21)* _ _ _ _ _ _ _ _ a regular in the *(22)* _ _ _ _ side. He played *(23)* _ _ instrumental role as the *(24)* _ _ _ _ _ _ _ States surged to the *(25)* _ _ _ _ _ _ _ _ _ _ _ _ global final at the 2009 *(26)* _ _ _ _ _ Confederations Cup in *(27)* _ _ _ _ _ _ Africa.

Michael Bradley played a *(28)* _ _ _ role in the USA *(29)* _ _ _ _ _ _ _ _ _ _ _ _ _ _ for the 2010 FIFA *(30)* _ _ _ _ _ _ Cup. He was *(31)* _ _ _ _ _ of the USA *(32)* _ _ _ _ _ that qualified for the 2010 FIFA World *(33)* _ _ _ and played an *(34)* _ _ _ _ _ _ _ _ _ _ _ _ _ _ role as the United States *(35)* _ _ _ _ _ _ _ to the 16th round. *(36)* _ _ part of the *(37)* _ _ squad for South *(38)* _ _ _ _ _ _ _ 2010 FIFA World Cup, *(39)* _ _ _ _ _ _ _ _ Bradley was coached *(40)* _ _ his own father *(41)* _ _ _ Bradley.

(Answer ID # 0842035)

1.	2.	3.
4.	5.	6.
7.	8.	9.
10.	11.	12.
13.	14.	15.
.16.	17.	18.
19.	20.	21.
22.	23.	24.
25.	26.	27.
28.	29.	30.
31.	32.	33.
34.	35.	36.
37.	38.	39.
40.	41.	

Lesson 12
DaMarcus Beasley

Answer Key 0475009
Word Bank

Academy	U-17	he	semi-finals
American	USA's	in	shining
Beasley	United	is	soccer
Chicago	World	join	summer
DaMarcus	Zealand	junior	team
FIFA	a	later	the
He	adidas	leaving	to
High	and	most	was
Los	at	pace	way
MLS	become	player	with
New	caught	recognized	years
Scotland	excelled	score	
Soccer	excelling	seek	

Directions: Fill in each blank with a word from the word bank that best completes the story.

DaMarcus Lamont Beasley *(1)* _____ an American soccer *(2)* _____ who played for *(3)* _____ United States soccer *(4)* _____ at South Africa 2010 *(5)* _____ Rangers FC of *(6)* _____.

DaMarcus Beasley played *(7)* _____ at South Side *(8)* _____ School for two *(9)* _____. He then moved *(10)* _____ Bradenton, Florida to *(11)* _____ the IMG Soccer *(12)* _____, the United States *(13)* _____ Federation's Residency program. *(14)* _____ signed with the *(15)* _____ Angeles Galaxy of *(16)* _____ on March 16, 1999. However, *(17)* _____ did not play *(18)* _____ single game until he *(19)* _____ traded to the *(20)* _____ Fire, with whom he *(21)* _____ from his debut *(22)* _____ 2000. Beasley would soon *(23)* _____ one of the *(24)* _____ prominent players in MLS and *(25)* _____ one of the *(26)* _____ States' European-based trailblazers. *(27)* _____ was a regular *(28)* _____ Chicago Fire before *(29)* _____ to Europe to *(30)* _____ his fortune.

DaMarcus Beasley *(31)* _____ fire straight away in Chicago, *(32)* _____ with his blistering *(33)* _____ and ability to *(34)* _____ and create goals. *(35)* _____ Beasley's emergence on the *(36)* _____ soccer scene started *(37)* _____ back in 2000, after *(38)* _____ for the USA's *(39)* _____ national team at the *(40)* _____ FIFA World Cup in *(41)* _____ Zealand in the *(42)* _____. He picked up the *(43)* _____ silver ball in the *(44)* _____ U-17 national team *(45)* _____ the junior FIFA *(46)* _____ Cup in New *(47)* _____ run to the *(48)* _____. Beasley was widely *(49)* _____ as the junior *(50)* _____ World Cup in New Zealand competition's best player behind only his then teammate, Landon Donovan. By 2000 Beasley was a force in the line up for Chicago Fire of Major League Soccer.

(Answer ID # 0475009)

1.	2.	3.
4.	5.	6.
7.	8.	9.
10.	11.	12.
13.	14.	15.
16.	17.	18.
19.	20.	21.
22.	23.	24.
25.	26.	27.
28.	29.	30.
31.	32.	33.
34.	35.	36.
37.	38.	39.

40.	41.	42.
43.	44.	45.
46.	47.	48.
49.	50.	

Answer Key 0841321
Word Bank

After	States	heavyweights	serious
Beasley	UEFA	in	side
Championship	US	international	team
DaMarcus	against	loan	the
December	and	loaned	then
Eindhoven	any	national	thus
Europe's	appearances	netted	to
He	at	occupies	today
January	before	of	was
June	cap	on	winner
Manchester	famous	score	with
Reyna	for	season	
Scottish	has	sent	

Directions: Fill in each blank with a word from the word bank that best completes the story.

DaMarcus Beasley played *(1)* _ _ _ the Under-20 team *(2)* _ _ the 2001 World Youth *(3)* _ _ _ _ _ _ _ _ _ _ _ _ in Argentina. DaMarcus *(4)* _ _ _ _ _ _ _ _ got his first *(5)* _ _ _ with the United *(6)* _ _ _ _ _ _ national team, on *(7)* _ _ _ _ _ _ _ _ 27, 2001 against China. By 2004 *(8)* _ _ _ _ _ _ _ _ _ Beasley's confidence was *(9)* _ _ display for all *(10)* _ _ see. With his *(11)* _ _ _ _ _ _ _ _ _ _ _ _ _ status rising through *(12)* _ _ _ _ _ _ _ _ _ _ _ with the US *(13)* _ _ _ _ _ _ _ _ team, DaMarcus Beasley *(14)* _ _ _ lured to Dutch *(15)* _ _ _ _ _ _ _ _ _ _ _ _ _ PSV Eindhoven by *(16)* _ _ _ _ _ coach Guus Hiddink *(17)* _ _ 2004. DaMarcus Beasley was *(18)* _ _ _ _ _ purchased by Dutch *(19)* _ _ _ _ _ PSV Eindhoven in *(20)* _ _ _ 2004 season. He was then *(21)* _ _ _ _ _ _ _ to Manchester City in 2006, *(22)* _ _ _ _ later signed by *(23)* _ _ _ _ _ _ _ _ _ giants Glasgow Rangers for £700,000 in *(24)* _ _ _ _ 2007, where he still *(25)* _ _ _ _ _ _ _ _ _ the left flank *(26)* _ _ midfield today. As of *(27)* _ _ _ _ _ _ July 2010, DaMarcus Beasley *(28)* _ _ _ scored more goals in *(29)* _ _ _ _ _ _ _ _ highest club competition, the *(30)* _ _ _ _ Champions League, than *(31)* _ _ _ other American player.

64

(32) _ _ _ _ _ _ contending with a *(33)* _ _ _ _ _ _ _ knee injury, DaMarcus Beasley was *(34)* _ _ _ _ off on a *(35)* _ _ _ _ move to English *(36)* _ _ _ _ Manchester City in the 2006–2007 *(37)* _ _ _ _ _ _ becoming the second *(38)* _ _ player - after Claudio *(39)* _ _ _ _ _ - to pull on the *(40)* _ _ _ _ _ _ blue kit. On *(41)* _ _ _ _ _ _ _ _ _ 30, that season DaMarcus Beasley *(42)* _ _ _ _ _ _ his first goal for *(43)* _ _ _ _ _ _ _ _ _ _ _ City, a game *(44)* _ _ _ _ _ _ _ in the 83rd minute *(45)* _ _ _ _ _ _ _ West Ham United. *(46)* _ _ went on to *(47)* _ _ _ _ _ _ three times more *(48)* _ _ _ _ _ _ _ returning to PSV *(49)* _ _ _ _ _ _ _ _ _. Beasley made 22 appearances *(50)* _ _ _ _ Manchester City before heading back to PSV, and eventually moving on to Rangers in the Scottish Premier League later that year. On January 16, 2006, DaMarcus was fined €1,500 (US $1,852) for driving under the influence of alcohol. He would be suspended for the next three months, followed by a three month probationary period and also lose his Dutch driving privileges.

DaMarcus Beasley
(Answer ID # 0841321)

1.	2.	3.
4.	5.	6.
7.	8.	9.
10.	11.	12.
13.	14.	15.
16.	17.	18.
19.	20.	21.
22.	23.	24.
25.	26.	27.
28.	29.	30.
31.	32.	33.
34.	35.	36.

37.	38.	39.
40.	41.	42.
43.	44.	45.
46.	47.	48.
49.	50.	

Answer Key 0898820
Word Bank

American	Raphael	in	substituted
Beasley	Stuttgart	is	success
Champions	UEFA	match	team
During	a	play	the
FC	competition	qualifier	to
League	first	score	while
Lowlands	freely	season	
Rangers	him	semi-final	

Directions: Fill in each blank with a word from the word bank that best completes the story.

Beasley scored his *(1) SIRFT* _____ goal for Rangers *(2) FC* _____ against FK Zeta *(3) IN* _____ a Champions League *(4) UEIRIAFQL* _____ on August 7, 2007, becoming *(5) HTE* _____ first American to *(6) OERSC* _____ for two clubs in the *(7) MTITPICOONE* _____. On October 2, 2007, DaMarcus *(8) YAELSBE* _____ was influential in *(9) ERRNSGA* _____ 3–0 win against Lyon in the *(10) ASICMPNHO* _____ League group stage. *(11) RDUNIG* _____ a UEFA Champions *(12) LGAUEE* _____ match against VfB *(13) RTAGTTSTU* _____, Beasley was hurt in *(14) A* _____ collision with goalkeeper *(15) HPELRAA* _____ Schäfer. This left *(16) IHM* _____ unable to complete the *(17) CTMAH* _____ and he was *(18) TTBDSESUUIT* _____. DaMarcus Beasley's first *(19) SENOSA* _____ with PSV Eindhoven in the *(20) ADLOLNWS* _____ was a big *(21) CESSCUS* _____ though. He scored *(22) EFLEYR* _____ and helped PSV *(23) TO* _____ a domestic title, *(24) IELWH* _____ also becoming the first *(25) CRMIENAA* _____ to line up in the *(26) IFINLS-MAE* _____ stages of the *(27) FAEU* _____ Champions League. DaMarcus Beasley *(28) IS* _____ the second American to *(29) LAYP* _____ for the Rangers' first *(30) TEMA* _____, after Claudio Reyna.

66

(Answer ID # 0898820)

1.	2.	3.
4.	5.	6.
7.	8.	9.
10.	11.	12.
13.	14.	15.
16.	17.	18.
19.	20.	21.
22.	23.	24.
25.	26.	27.
28.	29.	30.

Answer Key 0385657
Word Bank

Beasley	an	his	peak
CONCACAF	and	in	performer
Cup	as	international	repeated
DaMarcus	ball	is	round
He	called	jersey	side
New	cap	jinking	the
S	credit	matches	three
South	first	national	was
US	has	occasions	when
While	have	of	
also	having	pace	

Directions: Fill in each blank with a word from the word bank that best completes the story.

DaMarcus Beasley's first *(1) PAC* _____ for the US *(2) AINAONTL* _____ team came in 2001 *(3) WNEH* _____ he was only 19. *(4) RAAUMCSD* _____ Beasley was part *(5) OF* _____ the senior U.*(6) S* _____. squad that finished *(7) IN* _____ the quarterfinals of *(8) HTE* _____ 2002 FIFA World Cup, *(9) IVHANG* _____ played in all *(10) TEEHR* _____ group stage matches. DaMarcus *(11) SLYBEEA* _____ was a member of the *(12) US* _____ side that won the *(13) CACONAFC* _____ Gold Cup on three *(14) CONACOSIS* _____ (2002, 2005 and 2007). DaMarcus Beasley *(15) WSA* _____ a member of the US *(16) SEDI* _____ that went out in the *(17) STIFR* _____ round at Germany 2006 *(18) AN* _____ achievement that was *(19) PEEEDRTA* _____ at South Africa 2010. DaMarcus Beasley was *(20) LSOA* _____ part of the *(21) TUHSO* _____ Africa 2010 FIFA World *(22) CPU* _____ squad that reached *(23) DOUNR* _____ 16 and played all the *(24) TSAEHMC* _____. DaMarcus Beasley is *(25) LAECLD* _____ or nicknamed 'Jitterbug' for *(26) IHS* _____ deft tricks and *(27) IKJNGIN* _____ moves with the *(28) LALB* _____ at his feet. *(29) HE* _____ possesses bags of *(30) ACEP* _____. Now at 27, he *(31) IS* _____ still in his *(32) KEAP* _____ having already registered 93 *(33) EANTTRNIANLIO* _____ caps to his *(34) DERTIC* _____ and scoring 17 goals. *(35) ILWEH* _____ his club fortunes *(36) EVHA* _____ been decidedly up *(37) NAD* _____ down, DaMarcus Beasley *(38) SAH* _____ been a consistent *(39) EFROREMRP* _____ in a USA *(40) YJERES* _____ since his heroics *(41) AS* _____ a young teen in *(42) WEN* _____ Zealand in 1999.

(Answer ID # 0385657)

1.	2.	3.
4.	5.	6.
7.	8.	9.
10.	11.	12.
13.	14.	15.
16.	17.	18.
19.	20.	21.
22.	23.	24.
25.	26.	27.

28.	29.	30.
31.	32.	33.
34.	35.	36.
37.	38.	39.
40.	41.	42.

Answer Key 0256607
Word Bank

American	Rangers	freely	season
Americans'	Raphael	he	semi-final
As	Stuttgart	him	senior
Beasley	UEFA	in	substituted
Beasley's	US	is	success
Champions	World	match	team
DaMarcus	a	national	that
During	came	of	the
European	cap	play	to
FC	competition	qualifier	when
Hiddink	earn	quarter-finals	while
League	eye	quarterfinals	
Lowlands	first	score	

Directions: Fill in each blank with a word from the word bank that best completes the story.

Beasley scored his (1) _____ goal for Rangers (2) _____ against FK Zeta (3) _____ a Champions League (4) _____ on August 7, 2007, becoming (5) _____ first American to (6) _____ for two clubs in the (7) _____. On October 2, 2007, DaMarcus (8) _____ was influential in (9) _____ 3–0 win against Lyon in the (10) _____ League group stage. (11) _____ a UEFA Champions (12) _____ match against VfB (13) _____, Beasley was hurt in (14) _____ collision with goalkeeper (15) _____ Schäfer. This left (16) _____ unable to complete the (17) _____ and he was (18) _____. DaMarcus Beasley's first (19) _____ with PSV Eindhoven in the (20) _____ was a big (21) _____ though. He scored (22) _____ and helped PSV (23) _____ a domestic title, (24) _____ also becoming the first (25) _____ to line up in the (26)

69

_____ stages of the *(27)* _____ Champions League. DaMarcus Beasley *(28)* _____ the second American to *(29)* _____ for the Rangers' first *(30)* _____, after Claudio Reyna.

(31) _____ a member of the *(32)* _____ senior team, DaMarcus *(33)* _____ international shining moment *(34)* _____ at the 2002 FIFA *(35)* _____ Cup Korea/Japan™ where *(36)* _____ ran riot in the *(37)* _____ run to the *(38)* _____. His feat caught the *(39)* _____ of PSV coach *(40)* _____ and the rest *(41)* _____ the watching world to *(42)* _____ him a place in *(43)* _____ football.

DaMarcus Beasley's first *(44)* _____ for the US *(45)* _____ team came in 2001 *(46)* _____ he was only 19. *(47)* _____ Beasley was part of the *(48)* _____ U.S. squad *(49)* _____ finished in the *(50)* _____ of the 2002 FIFA World Cup, having played in all three group stage matches. DaMarcus Beasley was a member of the US side that won the CONCACAF Gold Cup on three occasions (2002, 2005 and 2007). DaMarcus Beasley was a member of the US side that went out in the first round at Germany 2006 an achievement that was repeated at South Africa 2010.

(Answer ID # 0256607)

1.	2.	3.
4.	5.	6.
7.	8.	9.
10.	11.	12.
13.	14.	15.
16.	17.	18.
19.	20.	21.
22.	23.	24.
25.	26.	27.
28.	29.	30.
31.	32.	33.

34.	35.	36.
37.	38.	39.
40.	41.	42.
43.	44.	45.
46.	47.	48.
49.	50.	

Lesson 13
Clint Dempsey

Answer Key 0854589
Word Bank

American	ball	goals	team
FIFA	be	honors	the
Fulham	career	in	tournaments
Latin	carved	is	trailer
League	centre-forward	most	up
Nacogdoches	club	national	versatile
US	decorated	one	was
USA	exercise	playing	who
United	fight	second	wing
University	first	small	with
ability	for	soccer	year
an	genuine	strength	
and	goal	striker	

Directions: Fill in each blank with a word from the word bank that best completes the story.

Clint Dempsey is *(1)* _____ American soccer player *(2)* _____ played for the *(3)* _____ States national team *(4)* _____ English Premier League *(5)* _____ Fulham. Clint Dempsey *(6)* _____ one of US *(7)* _____ successful soccer players *(8)* _____ the English Premier *(9)* _____ with London side, *(10)* _____, and one of *(11)* _____ more colorful characters in the *(12)* _____ line-up. Clint Dempsey is *(13)* _____ of America's most *(14)* _____ soccer players. Dempsey *(15)* _____ elected the US *(16)* _____ team player of the *(17)* _____ award in 2006 and *(18)* _____ Soccer athlete of the year *(19)* _____ in 2007. As a *(20)* _____ for the US *(21)* _____, Dempsey's touch on the *(22)* _____ is his primary *(23)* _____. Dempsey is a *(24)* _____ attacking player for the US national *(25)* _____ team; he could *(26)* _____ used on either *(27)* _____ or as a *(28)* _____. He is known *(29)* _____ his ball skills *(30)* _____ an eye for *(31)* _____ and keen dribbling *(32)* _____. Dempsey is the *(33)* _____ American to score *(34)* _____ in two different *(35)* _____ World Cup finals *(36)* _____, in 2006 and 2010.

As an *(37)* _____ soccer player, currently, *(38)* _____ in England's top *(39)* _____, Clint Dempsey, has *(40)* _____ out a thriving *(41)* _____ playing off a *(42)* _____ centre-forward. Clint Dempsey *(43)* _____ began playing soccer with the *(44)* _____ America immigrant population in the *(45)* _____ Texas town of *(46)* _____, where he grew *(47)* _____ humbly in a *(48)* _____. He attended Furman *(49)* _____ as a health and *(50)* _____ major. He was a key player for the Paladins. In December 2006, Fulham offered MLS a $4 million transfer fee for Clint Dempsey, then the largest amount ever offered for an MLS player. Clint Dempsey won the highest individual honor in American soccer when he was named Honda Player of the Year for 2006, beating Fulham teammates Kasey Keller and Brian McBride in a poll of sportswriters.

Clint Dempsey
(Answer ID # 0854589)

1.	2.	3.
4.	5.	6.
7.	8.	9.
10.	11.	12.
13.	14.	15.
16.	17.	18.
19.	20.	21.
22.	23.	24.
25.	26.	27.
28.	29.	30.
31.	32.	33.
34.	35.	36.
37.	38.	39.
40.	41.	42.

43.	44.	45.
46.	47.	48.
49.	50.	

Answer Key 0141375
Word Bank

American	U	defeat	regular
Americans'	USA's	earned	scored
CONCACAF	World	fastest	second
Confederations	a	final	shot
Cup	ability	for	striker
Cups	and	goal	the
Dempsey	battling	his	to
FIFA	became	in	tournament
Germany	but	international	very
Ghana	career	more	was
June	chest	national	with
S	count	only	
States'	debut	qualifier	

Directions: Fill in each blank with a word from the word bank that best completes the story.

Clint Dempsey made *(1) SIH* _____ USA debut in 2004, *(2) HTE* _____ same year he *(3) EABCME* _____ a fan favorite *(4) ITHW* _____ Fulham. Clint Dempsey's *(5) EERCRA* _____ with the US *(6) LTAAIONN* _____ team has been *(7) ERYV* _____ impressive. Since his 2004 *(8) DUBET* _____ with Team USA, *(9) YDSEEMP* _____ has been a *(10) REURGLA* _____. He has not *(11) OYLN* _____ made a mark with his *(12) IIYTBLA* _____ on the ball *(13) BTU* _____ also with his *(14) NLITBAGT* _____ nature, always fighting *(15) FRO* _____ the cause. Clint Dempsey *(16) CEDORS* _____ the USA's only *(17) OGAL* _____ at the FIFA *(18) OLRDW* _____ Cup™ in Germany *(19) IN* _____ 2006, and won the *(20) CFOAACNC* _____ Gold Cup twice in 2005 *(21) DNA* _____ 2007. Clint Dempsey played *(22) A* _____ crucial role in the *(23) SASU'* _____ run to the *(24) INLAF* _____ of the FIFA *(25) CIRONDEAFTEOSN* _____ Cup in 2009.

Prior *(26) TO* _____ South Africa FIFA World *(27) UCP* _____ 2010 Clint Dempsey had *(28) EERNAD* _____ a creditable 17 goals in 59 *(29) TONIALEITARNN* _____ appearances (not all as a *(30) KESRIRT* _____ though). US will *(31) OCUNT* _____ on Dempsey, for *(32) EORM* _____ goals at FIFA World *(33) PSUC* _____. On May 2,

2006, Clint Dempsey *(34) SAW* _____ named to the *(35) U* _____.S. roster for the 2006 *(36) IFFA* _____ World Cup tournament in *(37) EMGRYAN* _____, where he was the only *(38) CIRANEMA* _____ player to score a goal in the *(39) RNTETNMAOU* _____ with his equalizing goal in the *(40) MA'RASNCIE* _____ eventual 2–1 loss to *(41) GNHAA* _____. In the United *(42) TSATE'S* _____ opening 2010 World Cup *(43) QIEURALIF* _____, Clint Dempsey recorded the *(44) EAFTSST* _____ goal in U.*(45) S* _____. qualifying history with a *(46) CTSHE* _____ trap and sliding *(47) THOS* _____ 53 seconds into a 8–0 *(48) DETFEA* _____ of Barbados. On *(49) JNUE* _____ 12, 2010, Dempsey became the *(50) SCNDEO* _____ American (after Brian McBride) to score in more than one World Cup when he scored the equalizer goal against England in Americas' first game of the 2010 FIFA World Cup after the English goalkeeper Robert Green made a major error. Clint Dempsey is widely known for his second career as hip-hop artist 'Deuce.'

(Answer ID # 0141375)

1.	2.	3.
4.	5.	6.
7.	8.	9.
10.	11.	12.
13.	14.	15.
16.	17.	18.
19.	20.	21.
22.	23.	24.
25.	26.	27.
28.	29.	30.
31.	32.	33.
34.	35.	36.
37.	38.	39.

40.	41.	42.
43.	44.	45.
46.	47.	48.
49.	50.	

Answer Key 0813336
Word Bank

American	South	himself	scored
Atlético	a	his	suffered
August	after	in	the
Clint	and	injury	to
Dempsey	became	made	top
Diego	competition	major	vital
Eastlands	contract	match	was
Europa	defeat	minute	win
Fulham's	first	of	winning
He	for	on	with
Match	formed	only	won
On	goal	over	
Season	he	play	

Directions: Fill in each blank with a word from the word bank that best completes the story.

On May 5, 2007, Clint *(1)* _ _ _ _ _ _ _ scored his first *(2)* _ _ _ only goal of *(3)* _ _ _ 2006–07 season against Liverpool *(4)* _ _ _ _ _ coming on as *(5)* _ 54th minute substitute. Fulham *(6)* _ _ _ 1–0. This was a *(7)* _ _ _ _ _ and crucial win *(8)* _ _ _ Fulham as Dempsey's *(9)* _ _ _ _ would ensure Fulham's *(10)* _ _ _ flight status for the 2007–08 *(11)* _ _ _ _ _ _. On April 12, 2009, Dempsey *(12)* _ _ _ voted Man of the *(13)* _ _ _ _ _ in a 3–1 win *(14)* _ _ _ _ Manchester City at *(15)* _ _ _ _ _ _ _ _ _, in which he *(16)* _ _ _ _ _ _ two goals. On *(17)* _ _ _ _ _ _ 13, 2009, Dempsey signed a *(18)* _ _ _ _ _ _ _ _ extension to remain *(19)* _ _ _ _ Fulham through 2013. On August 20, 2009, *(20)* _ _ _ _ _ Dempsey scored his *(21)* _ _ _ _ _ goal in European *(22)* _ _ _ _ _ _ _ _ _ _ _, in the newly *(23)* _ _ _ _ _ _ Europa League, netting *(24)* _ _ _ _ _ _ _ _ second goal in a 3–1 *(25)* _ _ _ against Amkar Perm *(26)* _ _ the play-off round.

76

(27) _ _ January 17, 2010, Clint Dempsey *(28)* _ _ _ _ _ _ _ _ _ a cruciate ligament *(29)* _ _ _ _ _ _ in a 2–0 away *(30)* _ _ _ _ _ _ to Blackburn Rovers. *(31)* _ _ stayed out of *(32)* _ _ _ _ for two months; *(33)* _ _ _ _ _ to resume play *(34)* _ _ March 11, 2010 early enough *(35)* _ _ join the Ussquad for *(36)* _ _ _ _ _ Africa 2010. On May 12, 2010, Clint Dempsey *(37)* _ _ _ _ _ _ _ the first ever *(38)* _ _ _ _ _ _ _ _ _ to appear in a *(39)* _ _ _ _ _ European final, when *(40)* _ _ replaced Bobby Zamora in the 55th *(41)* _ _ _ _ _ _ _ of the 2010 UEFA *(42)* _ _ _ _ _ _ _ League Final. Unfortunately, *(43)* _ _ _ team, Fulham lost the *(44)* _ _ _ _ _ to, Atlético Madrid. *(45)* _ _ _ _ _ _ Forlán scored the *(46)* _ _ _ _ _ _ _ _ goal in the 116th minute *(47)* _ _ extra time, giving *(48)* _ _ _ _ _ _ _ _ _ a 2-1 win.

Clint Dempsey *(49)* _ _ _ _ a name for *(50)* _ _ _ _ _ _ _ _ in Major League Soccer, first lining up for the Boston-based New England Revolution in 2004.

(Answer ID # 0813336)

1.	2.	3.
4.	5.	6.
7.	8.	9.
10.	11.	12.
13.	14.	15.
16.	17.	18.
19.	20.	21.
22.	23.	24.
25.	26.	27.
28.	29.	30.
31.	32.	33.
34.	35.	36.
37.	38.	39.

40.	41.	42.
43.	44.	45.
46.	47.	48.
49.	50.	

Team USA 2010

Lesson 14
Landon Donovan

Word Bank

Academy	U-17	for	soon
American	United	forward	team
Donovan	a	has	the
FIFA	an	his	to
Galaxy	attended	in	too
Golden	back	join	top
In	best	made	tournament
Landon	by	national	training
Leverkusen	caps	one	twelve
Los	club	part	was
Major	contract	season	who
San	finished	signing	
Soccer's	first	skilful	

Directions: Fill in each blank with a word from the word bank that best completes the story.

   Landon Donovan is *(1)* _ _ _ _ _ _ _ _ attacking midfielder for *(2)* _ _ _ US national team *(3)* _ _ _ also plays for *(4)* _ _ _ Angeles Galaxy in *(5)* _ _ _ _ _ League Soccer. As *(6)* _ gifted player, Landon *(7)* _ _ _ _ _ _ _ _ _ is blessed with *(8)* _ _ ability to press *(9)* _ _ _ _ _ _ _ _ and get goals *(10)* _ _ the bag-load. In *(11)* _ _ _ _ first season with the *(12)* _ _ _ _ _ _, Landon Donovan scored *(13)* _ _ _ _ _ _ _ league goals and *(14)* _ _ _ _ _ ten assists. In 1999 *(15)* _ _ _ _ _ _ _ Donovan picked up the *(16)* _ _ _ _ _ _ _ Ball as the *(17)* _ _ _ _ _ player at the *(18)* _ _ _ _ _ U-17 World Championship *(19)* _ _ New Zealand and *(20)* _ _ _ _ _ afterwards earned his *(21)* _ _ _ _ _ _ call-up to a *(22)* _ _ _ _ _ _ _ States national team *(23)* _ _ _ _ _ _ _ _ _ _ camp. Landon Donovan, *(24)* _ _ _ since 1999 earned over 100 *(25)* _ _ _ _ and become USA's *(26)* _ _ _ _ all-time scorer. Landon Donovan *(27)* _ _ _ _ declared player of the *(28)* _ _ _ _ _ _ _ _ _ _ _ _ for his role in the *(29)* _ _ _ _ _ _ _ _ _ _ U-17 team that *(30)* _ _ _ _ _ _ _ _ _ fourth in the 1999 FIFA *(31)* _ _ _ _ _ World Championship, before *(32)* _ _ _ _ _ _ _ _ for Bayer Leverkusen.

   Donovan *(33)* _ _ _ _ _ _ _ _ _ the IMG Soccer *(34)* _ _ _ _ _ _ _ _ in Bradenton, Florida, *(35)* _ _ _ _ _ of U.S. *(36)* _ _ _ _ _ _ _ _ _ training program in 1999. *(37)* _ _ 1999 Landon Donovan became *(38)* _ _ _ of the youngest *(39)* _ _ _ _ _ _ _ _ _ players in history

79

(40) _ _ sign a professional *(41)* _ _ _ _ _ _ _ _ with an overseas *(42)* _ _ _ _ when he accepted to *(43)* _ _ _ _ German outfit Bayer *(44)* _ _ _ _ _ _ _ _ _ _. However, it proved *(45)* _ _ _ much pressure too soon *(46)* _ _ _ the youngster. After a *(47)* _ _ _ _ _ _ with Leverkusen's second *(48)* _ _ _ _, Donovan was sent *(49)* _ _ _ _ across the Atlantic to *(50)* _ _ _ Jose Earthquakes in a loan deal to allow him to gain more experience in the familiar surroundings of his home state of California. In his first season back from his unsuccessful German outfit, Bayer Leverkusen, Landon Donovan led his previously flagging Earthquakes to their first MLS championship in 2001.

Landon Donovan
(Answer ID # 0420258)

1.	2.	3.
4.	5.	6.
7.	8.	9.
10.	11.	12.
13.	14.	15.
16.	17.	18.
19.	20.	21.
22.	23.	24.
25.	26.	27.
28.	29.	30.
31.	32.	33.
34.	35.	36.
37.	38.	39.

40. _____	41. _____	42. _____
43. _____	44. _____	45. _____
46. _____	47. _____	48. _____
49. _____	50. _____	

Answer Key 0310027
Word Bank

Angeles	With	his	season
C	World	in	senior
Cup	a	league's	significant
Donovan	age	led	squad
In	an	loan	the
January	and	lost	top
Landon	at	named	tournament
Los	campaign	of	trained
MLS	coach	on	twice
Month	earned	pace	where
Munich	final	run	with
Premier	game	runner-up	
The	games	scored	

Directions: Fill in each blank with a word from the word bank that best completes the story.

In the 2007 SuperLiga *(1) NTUARNMOET* _____, Donovan was the *(2) TPO* _____ scorer. Donovan scored *(3) A* _____ goal in every *(4) MAGE* _____ except for the *(5) AFNLI* _____. In November 2008 Donovan *(6) RNDAETI* _____ with FC Bayern *(7) CHMNUI* _____, and later joined *(8) HTE* _____ German club on *(9) OANL* _____ until the start *(10) OF* _____ the 2009 MLS season *(11) IN* _____ mid-March. Playing along *(12) IHWT* _____ David Beckham at *(13) LSO* _____ Angeles Galaxy in 2009, *(14) VOADNNO* _____ enjoyed an outstanding 2009 *(15) IACPGMAN* _____. He won the *(16) AUELSE'G* _____ Most Valuable Player *(17) NAD* _____ MLS Goal of *(18) HTE* _____ Year 2009 award. As *(19) HSI* _____ club's captain, Landon Donovan *(20) DEL* _____ the Galaxy to *(21) MSL* _____ Cup 2009, which they *(22) TSLO* _____ on penalties. Landon Donovan led the Los *(23) GALSNEE* _____ Galaxy side to *(24) AN* _____ MLS crown in 2005 and a *(25) -NRENRUUP* _____ finish in 2009. After the 2009 MLS *(26) SSEANO* _____, Donovan joined English *(27) EMIREPR* _____ League side Everton *(28) ON* _____ loan in January 2010 *(29) WEEHR*

81

_____ he played thirteen *(30) GSMEA* _____ in all competitions and *(31) DCROSE* _____ two goals. In *(32) RJAYAUN* _____ 2009 at Everton F.*(33) C* _____., Landon Donovan was *(34) NMEDA* _____ the club's Player of the *(35) TNOHM* _____ for his performances in January.

(36) DLONAN _____ Donovan made his *(37) SRNOEI* _____ international debut in 2001. *(38) IHWT* _____ close control, explosive *(39) EPAC* _____ and superior vision, Landon Donovan *(40) REANED* _____ himself a place in *(41) OHACC* _____ Bruce Arena's regular *(42) DUAQS* _____ for the 2002 FIFA *(43) DRWLO* _____ Cup in Korea/Japan™ where, *(44) AT* _____ barely 20 years of *(45) AEG* _____, he played a *(46) TNIACIIGNFS* _____ role in USA's *(47) RNU* _____ to the quarter-finals. *(48) IN* _____ the 2002 FIFA World *(49) CPU* _____ in Korea Donovan scored *(50) CIETW* _____ in a successful campaign, against Poland in the first round and Mexico in their memorable Round of 16 feat. Landon Donovan was part of the US squad at Germany 2006 FIFA World Cup tournament and played a significant role for his team roaming between the midfield and attack until Ghana shockingly eliminated US.

(Answer ID # 0310027)

1.	2.	3.
4.	5.	6.
7.	8.	9.
10.	11.	12.
13.	14.	15.
16.	17.	18.
19.	20.	21.
22.	23.	24.
25.	26.	27.
28.	29.	30.
31.	32.	33.

34.	35.	36.
37.	38.	39.
40.	41.	42.
43.	44.	45.
46.	47.	48.
49.	50.	

Answer Key 0506480
Word Bank

Africa	active	game	six-time
As	all	have	the
Athlete	all-time	in	three-time
Donovan	and	is	through
Honda	as	most	to
Landon	award	of	vision
S	be	only	was
U	best	role	would
US	by	round	year
United	consecutive	score	
Year	explosive	scored	

Directions: Fill in each blank with a word from the word bank that best completes the story.

Donovan's close control, (1) _____ pace and superior (2) _____, played a significant (3) _____ in USA's run (4) _____ the round of 16 (5) _____ to be eliminated (6) _____ Ghana. At South (7) _____ 2010 FIFA World Cup (8) _____ 16, Landon Donovan took (9) _____ subsequent penalty and (10) _____ to tie the (11) _____ at 1-1, although Ghana (12) _____ later come back (13) _____ the first half (14) _____ extra time to score (15) _____ Asamoah Gyan, ending the (16) _____ 2-1.

Donovan is a (17) _____ winner of the (18) _____.S. Soccer Male (19) _____ of the Year (20) _____. As of July 2010, (21) _____ Donovan is the (22) _____ leader in scoring (23) _____ assists, for the (24) _____ States national team (25) _____ well as having the (26) _____ caps of all (27) _____ U.S. players. Landon (28) _____, as of July 2010 (29) _____ the only male to (30) _____ won the U.(31) _____. Soccer Male Athlete of the (32) _____ award in three (33) _____ years, as well as the only (34)

83

_____ winner of the *(35)* _____ Player of the Year award. *(36)* _____ a six-time winner of the *(37)* _____ player of the *(38)* _____ gong, Landon Donovan *(39)* _____ widely considered to *(40)* _____ one of the *(41)* _____ American players of *(42)* _____ time.

(Answer ID # 0506480)

1.	2.	3.
4.	5.	6.
7.	8.	9.
10.	11.	12.
13.	14.	15.
16.	17.	18.
19.	20.	21.
22.	23.	24.
25.	26.	27.
28.	29.	30.
31.	32.	33.
34.	35.	36.
37.	38.	39.
40.	41.	42.

**Lesson 15
Stuart Holden**

**Answer Key 0184176
Word Bank**

An	States	family	several
Bolton	Texan	for	side
Dynamo	US	his	soccer
English	Wanderers	in	team
He	a	made	the
Holden	after	making	time
Holden's	an	of	titles
It	attention	officially	two
Land	back	on	was
League	before	only	where
Major	club	player	would
Premier	directly	practicing	
Scotland	ended	set-up	

Directions: Fill in each blank with a word from the word bank that best completes the story.

Stuart Holden is *(1)* __ Scottish-born American soccer *(2)* _ _ _ _ _ _ _ who played for *(3)* _ _ _ _ United States national *(4)* _ _ _ _ _ and for Bolton *(5)* _ _ _ _ _ _ _ _ _ _ _ in the English *(6)* _ _ _ _ _ _ _ _ League.

Stuart Holden *(7)* _ _ _ born in Aberdeen, *(8)* _ _ _ _ _ _ _ _ _ and grew up *(9)* _ _ Sugar Land, Texas, *(10)* _ _ moved to Sugar *(11)* _ _ _ _ _, Texas, with his *(12)* _ _ _ _ _ _ _ when he was *(13)* _ _ _ _ 10. Stuart Holden played *(14)* _ _ _ years of college *(15)* _ _ _ _ _ _ _ at Clemson University *(16)* _ _ _ _ _ _ _ signing with English *(17)* _ _ _ _ Sunderland in March 2005. *(18)* _ _ ill-fated move to *(19)* _ _ _ _ _ _ _ _ side Sunderland in 2005 *(20)* _ _ _ _ _ without Stuart Holden *(21)* _ _ _ _ _ _ _ even one appearance *(22)* _ _ _ the club. Stuart *(23)* _ _ _ _ _ _ _ returned to the *(24)* _ _ _ _ _ _ _ from his unsuccessful English *(25)* _ _ _ _ _, Sunderland, to play in *(26)* _ _ _ _ _ _ League Soccer (MLS) with *(27)* _ _ _ _ hometown club Houston *(28)* _ _ _ _ _ _ _ for the 2006 season. *(29)* _ _ was in the Major *(30)* _ _ _ _ _ _ _ Soccer with Houston Dynamo, *(31)* _ _ _ _ _ _ Stuart Holden helped the *(32)* _ _ _ _ _ _ club to back-to-back *(33)* _ _ _ _ _ _ _ in 2006 and 2007. Stuart *(34)* _ _ _ _ _

85

_ _ _ _ performances at Houston Dynamo *(35)* _ _ _ _ _ soon caught the *(36)* _ _ _ _ _ _
_ _ _ of the authorities *(37)* _ _ the US national team *(38)* _ _ _ _ _ _ and also lead *(39)* _
_ _ _ _ _ _ _ to a move *(40)* _ _ _ _ to England; this *(41)* _ _ _ _ with Premier League
side *(42)* _ _ _ _ _ _ in January 2010. After *(43)* _ _ _ _ _ _ _ _ _ _ with them for
(44) _ _ _ _ _ _ weeks, Stuart Holden *(45)* _ _ _ _ _ _ _ _ _ _ joined Premier League
side Bolton Wanderers *(46)* _ _ January 25, 2010.

      Stuart Holden *(47)* _ _ _ _ his first appearance for the *(48)* _ _ senior side in 2009
(49) _ _ _ _ _ being named in *(50)* _ _ experimental line-up for that year's CONCACAF Gold
Cup, where US lost to Mexico in the final. Stuart Holden is able to play in an attacking-midfield
role or out wide on the right. Stuart Holden was named to the United States Gold Cup squad on
June 25, 2009. By June 2010, at 24, Stuart Holden had established himself as a versatile option
for Bob Bradley's US side ahead of the 2010 FIFA World Cup™. Stuart Holden has since 2009
picked up 13 caps for the full US national team and scored two goals.

Stuart Holden
(Answer ID # 0184176)

1.	2.	3.
4.	5.	6.
7.	8.	9.
10.	11.	12.
13.	14.	15.
16.	17.	18.
19.	20.	21.
22.	23.	24.
25.	26.	27.
28.	29.	30.
31.	32.	33.

34. _____	35. _____	36. _____
37. _____	38. _____	39. _____
40. _____	41. _____	42. _____
43. _____	44. _____	45. _____
46. _____	47. _____	48. _____
49. _____	50. _____	

Lesson 16
Ricardo Clark

Answer Key 0754661
Word Bank

After	Red	first	season
Atlanta	Ricardo	had	than
Bulls	South	he	the
Cup	United	his	to
Dynamo	York	in	useful
Earthquakes	a	location	where
Eintracht	an	member	who
Fußball-Bundesliga	and	moved	with
League	coach	park	year'
MetroStars	during	player	youthful
New	finalists	rest	

Directions: Fill in each blank with a word from the word bank that best completes the story.

Ricardo Clark is *(1)* _ _ American soccer player *(2)* _ _ _ played for the *(3)* _ _ _ _ _ _ States national team *(4)* _ _ _ also played for *(5)* _ _ _ _ _ _ _ _ _ Frankfurt in the *(6)* _. As a soccer *(7)* _ _ _ _ _ Ricardo Clark is *(8)* _ tireless worker in *(9)* _ _ _ middle of the *(10)* _ _ _ _. His exuberance, energy and *(11)* _ _ _ _ _ _ _ graft made him a *(12)* _ _ _ _ _ _ option for US *(13)* _ _ _ _ _, Bob Bradley at *(14)* _ _ _ _ _ _ Africa 2010 FIFA World *(15)* _ _ _.

Ricardo Clark, the *(16)* _ _ _ _ _ _ _ _, Georgia native began *(17)* _ _ _ professional career with the *(18)* _ _ _ _ _ _ _ _ _ _ (now the New York *(19)* _ _ _ Bulls) in 2003, where *(20)* _ _ was one of the *(21)* _ _ _ _ _ _ _ _ _ _ for the 'rookie of the *(22)* _ _ _ _ _ _ award in Major *(23)* _ _ _ _ _ _ Soccer. In his *(24)* _ _ _ _ _ year with the Red *(25)* _ _ _ _ _ _ in 2003, Ricardo Clark *(26)* _ _ _ a confident opening *(27)* _ _ _ _ _ _ _ and turned more *(28)* _ _ _ _ _ a few heads *(29)* _ _ the Big Apple *(30)* _ _ _ _ _ _ his professional career *(31)* _ _ _ _ _ the then MetroStars (now the *(32)* _ _ _ York Red Bulls). *(33)* _ _ _ _ _ _ becoming a regular *(34)* _ _ _ _ _ _ _ of the New *(35)* _ _ _ _ _ Red Bulls squad, *(36)* _ _ _ _ _ _ _ _ Clark was transferred *(37)* _ _ the San Jose *(38)* _ _ _ _ _ _ _ _ _ _ _ _ in 2005. He then *(39)* _ _ _ _ _ _ again - with the *(40)* _ _ _ _ of the team in a *(41)* _ _ _ _ _ _ _ _ change to Houston, *(42)* _ _ _ _ _ they became the *(43)* _ _ _ _ _ _ - in 2006.

Ricardo Clark
(Answer ID # 0754661)

1.	2.	3.
4.	5.	6.
7.	8.	9.
10.	11.	12.
13.	14.	15.
16.	17.	18.
19.	20.	21.
22.	23.	24.
25.	26.	27.
28.	29.	30.
31.	32.	33.
34.	35.	36.
37.	38.	39.
40.	41.	42.
43.		

Answer Key 0944075
Word Bank

Africa	South	got	role
America	States	great	scored
Arab	Texas-based	had	side
CONCACAF	USA	his	team
Clark's	United	in	that
Confederations	Youth	much-lauded	the
Cup	a	on	titles
Eintracht	cap	performance	to
October	finished	play	win
Paraguay	goal	regular	

Directions: Fill in each blank with a word from the word bank that best completes the story.

It was with *(1)* _____ Dynamo in Texas *(2)* _____ Ricardo Clark began *(3)* _____ really stand out *(4)* _____ the holding midfield *(5)* _____, winning back-to-back MLS *(6)* _____ in 2006 and 2007. Ricardo *(7)* _____ performances, as a *(8)* _____ midfielder with his *(9)* _____ club, Dynamo, and *(10)* _____ outstanding turn with the *(11)* _____ at the FIFA *(12)* _____ Cup in South *(13)* _____ in 2009 earned him *(14)* _____ move to Germany, to *(15)* _____ with Bundesliga outfit *(16)* _____ Frankfurt.

Ricardo Clark *(17)* _____ his first senior *(18)* _____ with the United *(19)* _____ national team on *(20)* _____ 12, 2005 against Panama, and *(21)* _____ his first international *(22)* _____ on July 2, 2007 against *(23)* _____ in the 2007 Copa *(24)* _____. Ricardo Clark went *(25)* _____ to be a *(26)* _____ in Bob Bradley's *(27)* _____, not only at the Confederations *(28)* _____ in 2007, where his *(29)* _____ in the fairytale *(30)* _____ over Spain was *(31)* _____ but also in *(32)* _____ Africa 2010 qualifying, where the USA *(33)* _____ first in the *(34)* _____ zone. Ricardo Clark *(35)* _____ played for the *(36)* _____ States national youth *(37)* _____ including the 2003 World *(38)* _____ Championship in the United *(39)* _____ Emirates

(Answer ID # 0944075)

1. _____	2. _____	3. _____
4. _____	5. _____	6. _____
7. _____	8. _____	9. _____
10. _____	11. _____	12. _____

13. _____	14. _____	15. _____
16. _____	17. _____	18. _____
19. _____	20. _____	21. _____
22. _____	23. _____	24. _____
25. _____	26. _____	27. _____
28. _____	29. _____	30. _____
31. _____	32. _____	33. _____
34. _____	35. _____	36. _____
37. _____	38. _____	39. _____

Lesson 17
José Francisco Torres

Answer Key 0462871 Word Bank			
Africa	Torres	de	outfit'
American	United	games	play
As	World	he	player
His	a	his	state
October	as	in	still
Pachuca	at	is	team
Team	broke	line-up	the
Texas	by	of	was

Directions: Fill in each blank with a word from the word bank that best completes the story.

José Francisco Torres *(1)* _ _ an American soccer *(2)* _ _ _ _ _ _ who played as *(3)* _ midfielder for Pachuca *(4)* _ _ the Primera División *(5)* _ _ México and the *(6)* _ _ _ _ _ _ States national team. *(7)* _ _ a versatile midfielder in *(8)* _ _ _ _ US national soccer *(9)* _ _ _ _, Francisco Torres made *(10)* _ _ _ _ appearance at South *(11)* _ _ _ _ _ _ 2010 FIFA World Cup. *(12)* _ _ _ first cap for *(13)* _ _ _ _ _ USA was on *(14)* _ _ _ _ _ _ _ _ 11, 2008 against Cuba.

Born in the *(15)* _ _ _ _ _ _ of Texas, Francisco *(16)* _ _ _ _ _ _ _ is the son *(17)* _ _ mixed Mexican and *(18)* _ _ _ _ _ _ _ _ _ parentage. Francisco Torres *(19)* _ _ _ _ recruited early on *(20)* _ _ a teenager to *(21)* _ _ _ _ _ for Mexican outfit *(22)* _ _ _ _ _ _ _ _ _. He was recruited *(23)* _ _ Pachuca while he was *(24)* _ _ _ _ _ _ attending high school in *(25)* _ _ _ _ _. Francisco Torres eventually *(26)* _ _ _ _ _ _ into the starting *(27)* _ _ _ _ _ _ _ _ for his Mexican *(28)* _ _ _ _ _ _ _ _ Pachuca, in 2008, where *(29)* _ _ played all three *(30)* _ _ _ _ _ for the club *(31)* _ _ the FIFA Club *(32)* _ _ _ _ _ _ Cup in Japan.

José Francisco Torres
(Answer ID # 0462871)

1.	2.	3.

4. _____	5. _____	6. _____
7. _____	8. _____	9. _____
10. _____	11. _____	12. _____
13. _____	14. _____	15. _____
16. _____	17. _____	18. _____
19. _____	20. _____	21. _____
22. _____	23. _____	24. _____
25. _____	26. _____	27. _____
28. _____	29. _____	30. _____
31. _____	32. _____	

Answer Key 0272309
Word Bank

Africa	Philadelphia	final	plays
Americans	Torres	for	professional
At	Tri	has	side
Beijing	U-23	he	the
Coach	US	his	to
Confederations	United	in	turned
Far	a	it	useful
League	accepted	join	was
Nowak	debut	lining	
Olympic	either	national	
On	eligible	not	

Directions: Fill in each blank with a word from the word bank that best completes the story.

Francisco Torres was *(1)* _____ to play for *(2)* _____ USA or Mexico. *(3)* _____ the

2008 Summer Olympics *(4)* _____ Beijing, Francisco Torres *(5)* _____ invited by Peter *(6)* _____, a Polish former *(7)* _____ soccer player and *(8)* _____ head coach of the *(9)* _____ Union in Major *(10)* _____ Soccer, to play *(11)* _____ the United States *(12)* _____ team but he *(13)* _____ down the opportunity *(14)* _____ play with the *(15)* _____ at the 2008 Beijing *(16)* _____ Games. It was *(17)* _____ until after the 2008 *(18)* _____ Olympic Games in the *(19)* _____ East that Francisco *(20)* _____ pledged his loyalty to the *(21)* _____ States. Even then *(22)* _____ looked as if *(23)* _____ was leaning towards *(24)* _____ up for El *(25)* _____, until late 2008 when he *(26)* _____ the invitation from *(27)* _____ Bob Bradley to *(28)* _____ the US camp. *(29)* _____ October 11, 2008, he made *(30)* _____ full national team *(31)* _____ against Cuba and *(32)* _____ since become a *(33)* _____ option in the *(34)* _____ line-up. Francisco Torres was *(35)* _____ part of the *(36)* _____ squad that reached the *(37)* _____ of the FIFA *(38)* _____ Cup in South *(39)* _____ in 2009, playing usually *(40)* _____ on the left *(41)* _____ of midfield.

(Answer ID # 0272309)

1.	2.	3.
4.	5.	6.
7.	8.	9.
10.	11.	12.
13.	14.	15.
16.	17.	18.
19.	20.	21.
22.	23.	24.
25.	26.	27.
28.	29.	30.
31.	32.	33.
34.	35.	36.

37.	38.	39.
40.	41.	

Lesson 18
Maurice Edu

Answer Key 1089062
Word Bank

California	Rangers	league's	seventy-fifth
College	Scottish	mathematics	short
Edu	Sr	midfielder	team
FC	a	mother	the
Kansas	an	naïve	university
League	award	notice	was
MLS	clubs	of	where
Maryland	debut	on	which
Maurice	game	overall	won
Nigeria	goal	part	year'
North	his	played	
Park	in	scored	

Directions: Fill in each blank with a word from the word bank that best completes the story.

Maurice Edu is (1) _____ American international soccer (2) _____, who played for (3) _____ FC in the (4) _____ First Division and (5) _____ United States national (6) _____.

Born in Fontana, (7) _____, Edu grew up (8) _____ San Bernardino, California (9) _____ his father, Maurice (10) _____., a native of (11) _____, worked as a (12) _____ teacher. Maurice Edu's (13) _____ who is also (14) _____ science teacher is a (15) _____ of Nigeria. Maurice (16) _____ attended the University (17) _____ Maryland at College (18) _____ from 2004 until 2006 and (19) _____ three years for the (20) _____ Terrapins. He was (21) _____ of the 2005 squad (22) _____ won the NCAA (23) _____ Cup national championship. (24) _____ Edu, however, cut (25) _____ his time at (26) _____ to join Major (27) _____ Soccer.

In 2007 Maurice Edu (28) _____ drafted by Toronto (29) _____ as the first (30) _____ pick of the 2007 (31) _____ SuperDraft. He made (32) _____ Major League Soccer (33) _____ on 25 April 2007, against (34) _____ City Wizards. Maurice Edu (35) _____ his first professional (36) _____ against Chicago Fire (37) _____ May 12, 2007 in the (38) _____ minute of the (39) _____. In 2008 Maurice Edu (40) _____

96

the North American *(41)* _____ 'rookie of the year' *(42)* _____. When Maurice Edu won the *(43)* _____ American league's 'rookie of the *(44)* _____ award some big-name *(45)* _____ of Europe took *(46)* _____ of him.

(Answer ID # 1089062)

1.	2.	3.
4.	5.	6.
7.	8.	9.
10.	11.	12.
13.	14.	15.
16.	17.	18.
19.	20.	21.
22.	23.	24.
25.	26.	27.
28.	29.	30.
31.	32.	33.
34.	35.	36.
37.	38.	39.
40.	41.	42.
43.	44.	45.
46.		

Answer Key 0891375
Word Bank

Czech	Steve	for	qualifying
Edu	Team	goal	re-established
El	United	his	registered
Glasgow	World	in	scored
Hibernian	against	international	signed
In	agreed	later	since
Maurice	at	many	stoppage-time
October	battled	obtaining	the
Rangers	cap	of	then
Scotland	during	officially	up
Since	fee	on	with
South	first	only	won

Directions: Fill in each blank with a word from the word bank that best completes the story.

On August 16, 2008, Maurice *(1)* _ _ _ arrived in Glasgow, *(2)* _ _ _ _ _ _ _ _ _ to hold talks *(3)* _ _ _ _ Rangers after a *(4)* _ _ _ of £2.6 million, was *(5)* _ _ _ _ _ _ with MLS. Maurice Edu *(6)* _ _ _ _ _ _ a five-year contract with *(7)* _ _ _ _ _ _ _ on August 17, 2008, and *(8)* _ _ _ _ _ _ _ _ _ _ _ joined the team *(9)* _ _ August 22 after successfully *(10)* _ _ _ _ _ _ _ _ _ a work permit. *(11)* _ _ _ _ _ then, he has *(12)* _ _ _ _ _ _ _ _ numerous injuries and *(13)* _ _ _ _ _ _ _ _ _ _ _ _ _ _ himself in the *(14)* _ _ _ _ _ team at the *(15)* _ _ _ _ _ _ _ _ club. Maurice Edu *(16)* _ _ _ _ _ _ his first goal *(17)* _ _ _ Rangers on April 8, 2009, *(18)* _ _ a league match *(19)* _ _ _ _ _ _ _ _ St Mirren. He *(20)* _ _ _ _ followed his goal *(21)* _ _ with another against *(22)* _ _ _ _ _ _ _ _ _ _ in a 3–2 win *(23)* _ _ Easter Road 11 days *(24)* _ _ _ _ _ _.

Maurice Edu made his *(25)* _ _ _ _ _ _ _ _ _ _ _ _ _ debut for the *(26)* _ _ _ _ _ _ States against Switzerland on *(27)* _ _ _ _ _ _ _ _ 17, 2007. Maurice Edu has *(28)* _ _ _ _ _ 2007 made a number *(29)* _ _ appearances despite his *(30)* _ _ _ _ injury woes He *(31)* _ _ _ his second international *(32)* _ _ _ _ a month later against *(33)* _ _ _ _ _ _ Africa, where he *(34)* _ _ _ _ _ _ _ _ _ _ _ an assist on *(35)* _ _ _ _ _ Cherundolo's winning goal. *(36)* _ _ 2009, Maurice Edu made *(37)* _ _ _ _ one brief appearance for *(38)* _ _ _ _ USA as a *(39)* _ _ _ _ _ _ _ _ _ _ _ _ _ substitute in a *(40)* _ _ _ _ _ _ Cup qualifier against *(41)* _ _ Salvador. That was *(42)* _ _ _ solitary game in *(43)* _ _ _ final stage of *(44)* _ _ _ _ _ _ _ _ _ _ _ for South Africa 2010. *(45)* _ _ _ _ _ _ _ _ Edu scored his first international *(46)* _ _ _ _ for the US *(47)* _ _ _ _ _ _ a friendly against *(48)* _ _ _ _ _ Republic on May 25, 2010.

(Answer ID # 0891375)

1.	2.	3.
4.	5.	6.
7.	8.	9.
10.	11.	12.
13.	14.	15.
16.	17.	18.
19.	20.	21.
22.	23.	24.
25.	26.	27.
28.	29.	30.
31.	32.	33.
34.	35.	36.
37.	38.	39.
40.	41.	42.
43.	44.	45.
46.	47.	48.

Answer Key 0464418
Word Bank

Africa	a	from	the
Coach	apparent	go	to
Cup	as	goal	warrant
FIFA	at	greatest	was
Ghana	by	in	what
June	controversial	it	winner
South	deficit	like	
US	deny	nullified	
World	draw	of	

Directions: Fill in each blank with a word from the word bank that best completes the story.

Edu played mostly *(1) AS* _____ a substitute for *(2) HCCAO* _____ Bradley at South *(3) FAIRAC* _____ 2010. His only goal *(4) AT* _____ South Africa 2010 FIFA *(5) DOLWR* _____ Cup was denied *(6) BY* _____ referee Koman Coulibaly *(7) OF* _____ Mali for no *(8) ANRPATPE* _____ reason. In their *(9) IFFA* _____ World Cup campaign *(10) IN* _____ South Africa on *(11) NUJE* _____ 18, 2010 against Slovenia at *(12) EHT* _____ group stage, the *(13) US* _____ had come back *(14) FORM* _____ a two-goal, second-half *(15) CFTIEDI* _____ to stage their *(16) RASETTGE* _____ World Cup comeback *(17) TO* _____ earn a remarkable 2-2 *(18) RAWD* _____. Edu's last minute *(19) OLGA* _____ would have tallied the *(20) NRENWI* _____. However, it was *(21) IUEDFNILL* _____. Up to, today, *(22) IT* _____ is not clear as to *(23) THAW* _____ exactly happened to *(24) RRAANTW* _____ the denial. It *(25) SAW* _____ one of the *(26) RTSCRAIOEVONL* _____ decisions made by *(27) A* _____ match official at *(28) HUTOS* _____ Africa 2010 FIFA World *(29) UCP* _____. Maurice Edu wept *(30) LIEK* _____ a baby when *(31) NAGAH* _____ scored against the US (2-1) to *(32) YEND* _____ US the chance to *(33) GO* _____ past round 16 at the South Africa 2010 FIFA World Cup.

Maurice Edu
(Answer ID # 0464418)

1.	2.	3.
4.	5.	6.
7.	8.	9.
10.	11.	12.

13.	14.	15.
16.	17.	18.
19.	20.	21.
22.	23.	24.
25.	26.	27.
28.	29.	30.
31.	32.	33.

Lesson 19
Benny Feilhaber

Answer Key 0278583
Word Bank

AGF	University	in	soccer
Angeles	York	later	spent
Austria	age	local	squad
Benny	an	midfielder	started
Brazil	and	national	team
California	around	not	the
City	be	noticed	to
Danish	became	of	unusual
Feilhaber	by	out	was
His	collegiate	paternal	where
Scarsdale	de	regime	youth
U-12	first	school	
United	his	six	

Directions: Fill in each blank with a word from the word bank that best completes the story.

Benny Feilhaber is *(1)* _ _ American international soccer *(2)* _ _ _ _ _ _ _ _ _ _ _, who played for *(3)* _ _ _ Aarhus in the *(4)* _ _ _ _ _ _ First Division and *(5)* _ _ _ United States national *(6)* _ _ _ _ _. Benny Feilhaber is *(7)* _ _ Austrian-Jewish ancestry and *(8)* _ _ _ born in Rio *(9)* _ _ Janeiro. Benny Feilhaber's *(10)* _ _ _ _ _ _ _ _ grandfather emigrated from *(11)* _ _ _ _ _ _ _ _ to Brazil in 1938 *(12)* _ _ escape the Nazi *(13)* _ _ _ _ _ _ _. Benny Feilhaber was *(14)* _ _ _ _ years old when *(15)* _ _ _ family moved from *(16)* _ _ _ _ _ _ _ to settle in the *(17)* _ _ _ _ _ _ _ States. He then *(18)* _ _ _ _ _ _ approximately eight years *(19)* _ _ the New York *(20)* _ _ _ _ _ suburb of Scarsdale *(21)* _ _ _ _ _ _ he played for the *(22)* _ _ _ _ _ _ soccer team, the *(23)* _ _ _ _ _ _ _ _ _ _ Lightning.

Benny Feilhaber *(24)* _ _ _ _ _ _ _ _ playing organized youth *(25)* _ _ _ _ _ _ _ at an early *(26)* _ _ _ _. In 1996, as a *(27)* _ _ _ _ _ _ soccer player Benny *(28)* _ _ _ _ _ _ _ _ _ led his team *(29)* _ _ _ won the New *(30)* _ _ _ _ _ State Cup for the *(31)* _ _ _ _ _ division. Benny Feilhaber *(32)* _ _ _ _ _ _ enrolled at the *(33)* _ _ _ _ _ _ _ _ _ _ of California, Los *(34)* _ _ _ _ _ _ _ _, but he was *(35)* _ _ _ recruited to play soccer. *(36)* _ _ _ arrival at organized *(37)* _ _ _ _ _ _ _ _ _ _ _ football was very *(38)* _ _ _ _ _ _ _ _. It was only *(39)* _ _ chance that Benny Feilhaber was *(40)* _ _ _ _ _ _ _ kicking a ball *(41)* _ _ _ _ _ _ the University of *(42)* _ _ _ _ _ _ _ _ _ _ campus. He was *(43)* _ _ _ _ _ _ invited to try

(44) _ _ _ _ for the school team. *(45)* _ _ _ _ _ _ made the grade in the University of California *(46)* _ _ _ _ _ _ _ _ team and soon *(47)* _ _ _ _ _ _ _ a standout member of the *(48)* _ _ _ _ _ _. He would soon *(49)* _ _ called into USA's *(50)* _ _ _ _ _ _ _ _ _ youth team.

Benny Feilhaber
(Answer ID # 0278583)

1.	2.	3.
4.	5.	6.
7.	8.	9.
10.	11.	12.
13.	14.	15.
16.	17.	18.
19.	20.	21.
22.	23.	24.
25.	26.	27.
28.	29.	30.
31.	32.	33.
34.	35.	36.
37.	38.	39.
40.	41.	42.
43.	44.	45.
46.	47.	48.

49.	50.	
_____	_____	

Answer Key 1038494
Word Bank

AGF	On	for	settling
August	Premier	free	spending
Bundesliga	Schalke	in	stretch
Danish	World	made	substitute
Derby	a	moved	the
Feilhaber	after	on	then
Gymnastikforening	as	overall	third
Hamburg	at	relegated	to
He	club	reserves	work
League	coming	season	
Netherlands	eventually	second	

Directions: Fill in each blank with a word from the word bank that best completes the story.

After an outstanding *(1) OELARLV* _____ performance for USA *(2) AT* _____ the FIFA U-20 *(3) LDOWR* _____ Cup in the *(4) SLDEETANNRH* _____ in 2005, Bundesliga FC, *(5) BRHUMGA* _____ came calling and *(6) ETAENVULLY* _____ signed the 20-year-old Benny *(7) RFIAHEBLE* _____. Feilhaber signed for Hamburg *(8) IN* _____ July 2005. In the 2005–06 *(9) ANOSES* _____ Feilhaber played with *(10) EHT* _____ Hamburg reserve team in the *(11) TDHIR* _____ division (or Regionalliga). After *(12) GNISDPNE* _____ time with the *(13) ESRVESRE* _____ at Hamburg, Benny Feilhaber *(14) VDEMO* _____ on to join *(15) ULADSBNGIE* _____. On October 12, 2006, Feilhaber *(16) DMEA* _____ his Bundesliga debut, *(17) MGNOIC* _____ on as a *(18) DNOSCE* _____ half substitute in *(19) A* _____ 2–1 home loss to *(20) LCAHKSE* _____ 04. From Hamburg Benny Feilhaber moved *(21) ON* _____ to an unhappy *(22) HSTCTER* _____ at Derby County, *(23) EHTN* _____ of the English *(24) PRIERME* _____ League in 2007 before *(25) TSEGITNL* _____ in Denmark with *(26) GAF* _____ after Derby's relegation.

(27) ON _____ August 9, 2007, Feilhaber obtained a *(28) WKRO* _____ permit to play *(29) ROF* _____ newly promoted Premier *(30) LGEAEU* _____ side, Derby County. *(31) DEYBR* _____ FC released Feilhaber on a *(32) EERF* _____ transfer after being *(33) TEAELDGER* _____ from the Premier League *(34) EFART* _____ only one season. On *(35) TAUGUS* _____ 15, 2008, Feilhaber signed with *(36) IADHSN* _____ Superliga team, Aarhus *(37) GNNSTGERIAOMKIFYN* _____, commonly known as AGF. *(38) HE* _____ made his debut for AGF *(39) BCLU* _____ on September 1, 2008,

coming on *(40) AS* _____ a fifty-ninth minute *(41) STBESUUTIT* _____ in a 0–3 loss *(42) TO* _____ FC Nordsjælland.

(Answer ID # 1038494)

1.	2.	3.
4.	5.	6.
7.	8.	9.
10.	11.	12.
13.	14.	15.
16.	17.	18.
19.	20.	21.
22.	23.	24.
25.	26.	27.
28.	29.	30.
31.	32.	33.
34.	35.	36.
37.	38.	39.
40.	41.	42.

Answer Key 0601482
Word Bank

Africa	a	however	scored
CONCACAF	against	injuries	spite
Confederations	all	international	squad
Ecuador	as	managed	team
Feilhaber	caps	national	that
June	debut	of	the
Mexico	final	on	three
S	first	part	up
Summer	form	playing	was
U	had	playmaking	when
US	his	registered	with

Directions: Fill in each blank with a word from the word bank that best completes the story.

Feilhaber made his *(1)* _____ career start for *(2)* _____ U.S. senior *(3)* _____ on March 25, 2007, against *(4)* _____, and scored his first *(5)* _____ goal against China *(6)* _____ June 2, 2007. Despite series *(7)* _____ injuries in 2007 Feilhaber *(8)* _____ named to the *(9)* _____.S. Under-23 squad *(10)* _____ competed at the 2008 *(11)* _____ Olympics. He appeared *(12)* _____ a substitute in *(13)* _____ three games for the U.*(14)* _____. As integral part of the 23-man *(15)* _____ for the South *(16)* _____ 2010 FIFA World Cup, *(17)* _____ was used as *(18)* _____ substitute. He gained *(19)* _____ time in two of the *(20)* _____ group stage matches *(21)* _____ Slovenia where US *(22)* _____ a draw and *(23)* _____ Algeria where the *(24)* _____ won. An elegant *(25)* _____ midfielder though, Benny Feilhaber, *(26)* _____ suffered from niggling *(27)* _____ and lack of *(28)* _____ prior to South Africa 2010.

In *(29)* _____ of his injuries *(30)* _____, Benny Feilhaber has *(31)* _____ to pick up 31 *(32)* _____ since making his *(33)* _____ in the US *(34)* _____ team in 2007. By *(35)* _____ 2010, Benny Feilhaber had *(36)* _____ two goals, including *(37)* _____ golden long-range winner against *(38)* _____ in the final of the 2007 *(39)* _____ Gold Cup. Benny Feilhaber was *(40)* _____ of the line *(41)* _____ for the US *(42)* _____ they went to the *(43)* _____ of the 2009 FIFA *(44)* _____ Cup in South Africa.

(Answer ID # 0601482)

1. _____	2. _____	3. _____
4. _____	5. _____	6. _____

7.	8.	9.
10.	11.	12.
13.	14.	15.
16.	17.	18.
19.	20.	21.
22.	23.	24.
25.	26.	27.
28.	29.	30.
31.	32.	33.
34.	35.	36.
37.	38.	39.
40.	41.	42.
43.	44.	

Lesson 20
Herculez Gomez

Answer Key 1056206 Word Bank			
Angeles	States	competes	is
Clausura	a	de	lower
Colorado	an	decided	scorer
Cup	ancestry	earned	second
Durango	and	followed	the
Galaxy	appearances	football	to
Gomez	arts	for	until
Hunt	before	goal	when
MLS	began	his	where
Mexico	brother	in	who

Directions: Fill in each blank with a word from the word bank that best completes the story.

Herculez Gomez is *(1)* _ _ American soccer player *(2)* _ _ _ played for Pachuca *(3)* _ _ the Primera División *(4)* _ _ México. Herculez Gomez *(5)* _ _ of joint Mexican-American *(6)* _ _ _ _ _ _ _ _. He is the *(7)* _ _ _ _ _ _ _ of Mixed martial *(8)* _ _ _ _ (MMA) fighter Ulysses Gomez, *(9)* _ Mexican-American professional who *(10)* _ _ _ _ _ _ _ _ in the flyweight *(11)* _ _ _ bantamweight divisions.

Herculez Gomez *(12)* _ _ _ _ _ his club career in *(13)* _ _ _ _ _ _ _ _ where he played *(14)* _ _ _ a succession of *(15)* _ _ _ _ _ _ league teams in *(16)* _ _ _ _ _ _ _ before settling in *(17)* _ _ _ _ United States with *(18)* _ _ _ hometown club, Los *(19)* _ _ _ _ _ _ _ _ Galaxy in 2003. Herculez *(20)* _ _ _ _ _ scored the game-winning *(21)* _ _ _ _ _ in the 2005 Lamar *(22)* _ _ _ _ _ U.S. Open *(23)* _ _ _ Final. He helped the *(24)* _ _ _ _ _ _ _ to a rare Cup 'double' *(25)* _ _ _ _ they also won the 2005 *(26)* _ _ _ Cup. Unsuccessful stretches in *(27)* _ _ _ _ _ _ _ _ _ and Kansas City *(28)* _ _ _ _ _ _ _ _ _ _ before Herculez Gomez *(29)* _ _ _ _ _ _ _ _ to move back *(30)* _ _ Mexico and Puebla, *(31)* _ _ _ _ _ _ his 10 goals in 14 *(32)* _ _ _ _ _ _ _ _ _ _ _ _ for the club *(33)* _ _ _ _ _ _ _ him the top *(34)* _ _ _ _ _ _ _ title in the *(35)* _ _ _ _ _ _ _ _ _ _. He stayed in Mexico *(36)* _ _ _ _ _ 2006 and scored 16 goals in 53 appearances *(37)* _ _ _ _ _ _ _ being loaned out to the *(38)* _ _ _ _ _ _ tier of professional *(39)* _ _ _ _ _ _ _ _ _ _ in the United *(40)* _ _ _ _ _ _ _.

Herculez Gomez
(Answer ID # 1056206)

1.	2.	3.
4.	5.	6.
7.	8.	9.
10.	11.	12.
13.	14.	15.
16.	17.	18.
19.	20.	21.
22.	23.	24.
25.	26.	27.
28.	29.	30.
31.	32.	33.
34.	35.	36.
37.	38.	39.
40.		

Answer Key 0824378
Word Bank

Africa™	This	fourth	round
C	US	game	season
City	a	goal	signed
FIFA	club	goals	the
Gomez	doing	in	time

Herculez	exchange	lead	to
January	feat	led	was
Park	first	of	with
Puebla	for	pick	

Directions: Fill in each blank with a word from the word bank that best completes the story.

On December 1, 2006, Herculez *(1)* _____ was traded to *(2)* _____ Colorado Rapids along *(3)* _____ Ugo Ihemelu in *(4)* _____ for Joe Cannon. *(5)* _____ Gomez scored the *(6)* _____ goal in his first *(7)* _____ for Colorado, in *(8)* _____ 2-1 win over D.*(9)* _____. United on April 7, 2007. *(10)* _____ was the first *(11)* _____ in the history *(12)* _____ Dick's Sporting Goods *(13)* _____. On September 3, 2008, Herculez Gomez *(14)* _____ traded to Kansas *(15)* _____ Wizards in exchange *(16)* _____ allocation money, a *(17)* _____ round 2009 MLS SuperDraft *(18)* _____ and a first *(19)* _____ 2009 MLS Supplemental Draft pick. Herculez Gomez *(20)* _____ with Mexican club *(21)* _____ F.C. in *(22)* _____ 2010 and scored ten *(23)* _____ in the 2010 Mexican *(24)* _____ to tie for the *(25)* _____ for most goals; a *(26)* _____ which marked the first *(27)* _____ any American player *(28)* _____ a foreign league *(29)* _____ goals. By January 2010, Herculez Gomez was *(30)* _____ too well at *(31)* _____ level in Mexico *(32)* _____ be ignored by *(33)* _____ coach Bob Bradley for 2010 *(34)* _____ World Cup South *(35)* _____.

(Answer ID # 0824378)

1.	2.	3.
4.	5.	6.
7.	8.	9.
10.	11.	12.
13.	14.	15.
16.	17.	18.
19.	20.	21.
22.	23.	24.

25. _____	26. _____	27. _____
28. _____	29. _____	30. _____
31. _____	32. _____	33. _____
34. _____	35. _____	

[Answer Key 0319821]
Word Bank

Africa™	USA	encounter	of
Cup	World	first	scored
Czech	a	for	soccer
FIFA	and	game	spark
Herculez	any	games	substitute
On	bench	goal	the
S	cap	in	when
South	dangerous	make	
States	did	need	

Directions: Fill in each blank with a word from the word bank that best completes the story.

Herculez Gomez joined *(1) HTE* _____ United States national *(2) ESROCC* _____ team's roster in 2007 *(3) OFR* _____ the 2007 Copa America, *(4) DNA* _____ earned his first *(5) PAC* _____ as a second-half *(6) USITEUSBTT* _____ against Argentina. His *(7) STRIF* _____ start with Team *(8) UAS* _____ was against Colombia. *(9) ON* _____ May 25, 2010, Herculez Gomez *(10) ECSORD* _____ his first international *(11) GAOL* _____ for the U.*(12) S* _____. national team in *(13) A* _____ 4-2 friendly defeat to the *(14) CCZHE* _____ Republic. Herculez Gomez *(15) DDI* _____ not play in *(16) AYN* _____ of USA's qualifiers for *(17) HSUOT* _____ Africa 2010 and therefore 2010 *(18) AFFI* _____ World Cup South *(19) C™AFRIA* _____ was his first *(20) COETNNREU* _____ at a FIFA *(21) DOLWR* _____ Cup. He played *(22) IN* _____ 3 out of the 4 *(23) EMGAS* _____ for the United *(24) ASETTS* _____ at the 2010 FIFA World *(25) PUC* _____, including the round *(26) OF* _____ 16 game against Ghana. *(27) UCZLEERH* _____ Gomez's ability to *(28) AEMK* _____ an impact off the *(29) NECHB* _____ makes him a *(30) OUDAGNRSE* _____ weapon for Team USA *(31) HENW* _____ they find themselves in *(32) NEDE* _____ of an attacking *(33) SPAKR* _____ late in a *(34) EGAM* _____.

(Answer ID # 0319821)

1.	2.	3.
4.	5.	6.
7.	8.	9.
10.	11.	12.

112

13.	14.	15.
16.	17.	18.
19.	20.	21.
22.	23.	24.
25.	26.	27.
28.	29.	30.
31.	32.	33.
34.		

Lesson 21
Edson Buddle

Answer Key 0556646
Word Bank

Before	Red	for	starts
Buddle	Rough	goals	suspension
Columbus	Soccer	his	the
Crew	Toronto	home	then
Cup	York	in	three
Eddie	a	managed	to
FC	and	moved	traded
Leitch	assists	nine	two
MLS	brief	of	was
New	disappointing	previously	with
November	due	scoring	young
Ohio	established	significant	
On	foot	spite	

Directions: Fill in each blank with a word from the word bank that best completes the story.

Edson Buddle began *(1)* _ _ _ _ club career in *(2)* _ _ _ US lower leagues (A-League) *(3)* _ _ _ _ the Long Island *(4)* _ _ _ _ _ Riders in 2000. He *(5)* _ _ _ _ _ joined Major League *(6)* _ _ _ _ _ _ and played for *(7)* _ _ _ _ _ _ _ _ Crew from 2001 to 2005. *(8)* _ _ _ _ _ _ played only 556 minutes *(9)* _ _ his rookie year (2001) with the Columbus *(10)* _ _ _ _ but he managed *(11)* _ _ show his talent in his *(12)* _ _ _ _ _ playing time, scoring *(13)* _ _ _ _ _ _ goals and two *(14)* _ _ _ _ _ _ _ _. By 2002 Buddle had *(15)* _ _ _ _ _ _ _ _ _ _ _ himself as one *(16)* _ _ the league's best *(17)* _ _ _ _ _ _ strikers. He scored *(18)* _ _ _ helped the Columbus Crew to *(19)* _ U.S. Open *(20)* _ _ _ _ win. He scored 42 *(21)* _ _ _ _ _ in 101 appearances for the *(22)* _ _ _ _ _ club. From the Columbus Crew, Buddle *(23)* _ _ _ _ _ to New York *(24)* _ _ _ Bulls and later to *(25)* _ _ _ _ _ _ _ _ FC.

Edson Buddle missed *(26)* _ _ _ _ _ _ _ _ _ _ _ _ time of play in 2004 *(27)* _ _ _ _ injury, but still *(28)* _ _ _ _ _ _ _ _ _ to score eleven goals and *(29)* _ _ _ assists in twenty *(30)* _ _ _ _ _ _ _ _. He also totaled *(31)* _ _ _ _ Major League Soccer goals and two assists in 2005 in *(32)* _ _ _ _ _ _ of being on *(33)* _ _ _ _ _ _ _ _ _ _ _ for a month. *(34)* _ _ _ _ _ _ the 2006 season he *(35)* _ _ _ traded to New *(36)* _ _ _ _ Red Bull for *(37)* _ _ _ _ _ _ Gaven and Chris *(38)* _ _ _ _ _ _ _. Buddle had a *(39)* _ _ _ _ _ _ _ _ _ _ _ _ _ _ year with the *(40)* _ _ _ York Red Bull *(41)* _ _ _ _ _ _ _ _ only six goals due to a *(42)* _ _ _ _ injury in 2006. On *(43)* _ _ _ _ _ _ _ _ _ 22, 2006 Edson Buddle, thus, was *(44)* _ _ _ _ _ _ _ to Toronto FC *(45)* _ _ _ Tim Regan who was *(46)* _ _ _ _ _ _ _ _ _ _ claimed in the 2006 *(47)* _ _ _ Expansion Draft by Toronto *(48)* _ _. Edson Buddle finally found a *(49)* _ _ _ _ in Los Angeles in 2007.

Edson Buddle
(Answer ID # 0556646)

1.	2.	3.
4.	5.	6.
7.	8.	9.
10.	11.	12.
13.	14.	15.
16.	17.	18.
19.	20.	21.
22.	23.	24.
25.	26.	27.
28.	29.	30.
31.	32.	33.
34.	35.	36.
37.	38.	39.
40.	41.	42.
43.	44.	45.
46.	47.	48.

49.	50.	
_____	_____	

Answer Key 0186808
Word Bank

Buddle	a	is	striker
Buddle's	as	loss	take
Cup	club	national	the
FIFA	first	of	until
May	for	on	usually
Republic	friendly	or	was
South	had	preliminary	with
USA's	he	prominently	
United	hole	see	
World	in	since	

Directions: Fill in each blank with a word from the word bank that best completes the story.

Edson Buddle's resume *(1) HWIT* _____ the national team *(2) IS* _____ not as great *(3) AS* _____ with his MSL *(4) ULCB* _____. He earned his *(5) RITFS* _____ senior team cap *(6) ON* _____ March 29, 2003, in a *(7) FNELDYIR* _____ against Venezuela. On *(8) AMY* _____ 25, 2010, Edson Buddle started *(9) IN* _____ a 4-2 international friendly *(10) SOSL* _____ to the Czech *(11) BPIEUCLR* _____ but would not *(12) EES* _____ the field for *(13) TEH* _____ U.S. again *(14) NILUT* _____ South Africa 2010 when *(15) HE* _____ was named to the *(16) MEYIPRNARIL* _____ squad of the *(17) UDTNEI* _____ States national team *(18) FRO* _____ the 2010 World Cup.

Edson *(19) UDDBLE* _____ has only made *(20) A* _____ handful of appearances *(21) NCEIS* _____ 2003. He did not *(22) EAKT* _____ part in any *(23) OF* _____ the qualifiers for the 2010 *(24) OWLDR* _____ Cup. At 29, Buddle *(25) DAH* _____ yet to figure *(26) YEOMPNLRTNI* _____ in the US *(27) LNAIATON* _____ team set-up. He *(28) YLLSUAU* _____ fills in for *(29) OR* _____ substitutes Landon Donovan. *(30) THUOS* _____ Africa 2010 was Edson *(31) LUDSD'BE* _____ first run-out at a *(32) FIAF* _____ World Cup. He *(33) AWS* _____ a late addition in *(34) SSUA'* _____ squad to fill the *(35) EOLH* _____ left by injured *(36) IETRKSR* _____ Charlie Davies for the 2010 FIFA World *(37) UCP* _____ South Africa™.

116

(Answer ID # 0186808)

1.	2.	3.
4.	5.	6.
7.	8.	9.
10.	11.	12.
13.	14.	15.
16.	17.	18.
19.	20.	21.
22.	23.	24.
25.	26.	27.
28.	29.	30.
31.	32.	33.
34.	35.	36.
37.		

Answer Key 0594418
Word Bank

American	National	father	played
Buddle	Pelé	him	soccer
Los	State	is	that
Major	States	legend	the
Nascimento	and	of	was

Directions: Fill in each blank with a word from the word bank that best completes the story.

Edson Buddle is an *(1)* _____ soccer player who *(2)* _____ for the United *(3)* _____ national team and *(4)* _____ Angeles Galaxy in *(5)* _____ League Soccer.It *(6)* _____ interesting to note *(7)* _____ Edson's father named *(8)* _____ after Brazilian football *(9)* _____, Edson Arantes do *(10)* _____, better known as *(11)* _____. Winston Buddle, his *(12)* _____, born in Jamaica *(13)* _____ also a professional *(14)* _____ player himself. Edson *(15)* _____ played one year *(16)* _____ college soccer at *(17)* _____ Fair Community College *(18)* _____ led them to *(19)* _____ 1999 NJCAA Division I *(20)* _____ Championship.

(Answer ID # 0594418)

1.	2.	3.
4.	5.	6.
7.	8.	9.
10.	11.	12.
13.	14.	15.
16.	17.	18.
19.	20.	

Lesson 22
Jozy Altidore

Answer Key 0694352			
Word Bank			
Altidore	Real	goals	player
Altidore's	September	his	professional
American	Soccer	in	scored
Athletic	Spain's	leaders	season
August	York	loan	signed
Bulls	against	making	signing
C	aggregate	million	the
D	and	minute	top
La	at	not	two
Major	by	of	was
November	came	on	with
Open	fan	only	
Pellegrini	flights	opposition	

Directions: Fill in each blank with a word from the word bank that best completes the story.

Altidore began his *(1)* _ _ _ _ _ _ _ _ _ _ _ _ career at 19. He *(2)* _ _ _ _ _ _ for the MetroStars (now *(3)* _ _ _ New York Red *(4)* _ _ _ _ _ in 2006 and made *(5)* _ _ _ professional debut on *(6)* _ _ _ _ _ _ 23, 2006, as a substitute *(7)* _ _ a 3–1 U.S. *(8)* _ _ _ _ _ Cup loss to *(9)* _.C. United. On *(10)* _ _ _ _ _ _ _ _ _ 30, 2006, Altidore became a *(11)* _ _ _ favorite when he *(12)* _ _ _ _ _ _ _ the Red Bulls' *(13)* _ _ _ _ _ goal of their 2–1 *(14)* _ _ _ _ _ _ _ _ _ _ loss to D.*(15)* _ becoming the youngest *(16)* _ _ _ _ _ _ _ to score in the *(17)* _ _ _ _ _ _ League Soccer playoffs *(18)* _ _ 16 years. He scored 15 *(19)* _ _ _ _ _ _ in 37 appearances over *(20)* _ _ _ seasons for New *(21)* _ _ _ _ _ Red Bulls. Soon *(22)* _ _ _ _ _ _ _ _ _ _ _ hunger for goal *(23)* _ _ _ ability to disrupt *(24)* _ _ _ _ _ _ _ _ _ _ _ defences was noticed *(25)* _ _ one of Europe's *(26)* _ _ _ _ talent assessors, former *(27)* _ _ _ _ _ Madrid coach Manuel *(28)* _ _ _ _ _ _ _ _ _ _ _ _. Manuel Pellegrini brought *(29)* _ _ _ _ _ _ _ _ _ _ to La Liga, *(30)* _ _ _ _ _ Villarreal FC, one *(31)* _ _ Spain's ultra-competitive top *(32)* _ _ _ _ _ _ _ _ at the start of the 2008 *(33)* _ _ _ _ _ _ for a reported $10 *(34)* _ _ _ _ _ _ _ _ (€7.4 million), on June 4, 2008 *(35)* _ _ _ _ _ _ _ Altidore the biggest-ever *(36)* _ _ _ _ _ _ _ from Major League *(37)* _ _ _ _ _ _ _. Altidore first featured *(38)* _ _ _ _ _ _ _ _ Athletic Bilbao on *(39)* _ _ _ _ _ _ _ _ _ 1, 2008 becoming the first *(40)* _ _ _ _ _ _ _ _ international to score in *(41)* _ _ Liga when he *(42)* _ _ _ _ _ on in the 90th *(43)* _ _ _ _ _ _

119

and scored against *(44)* _ _ _ _ _ _ _ Bilbao. Unfortunately Altidore could *(45)* _ _ _ stay long in *(46)* _ _ _ _ _ _ _ top flight. He *(47)* _ _ _ sent out on *(48)* _ _ _ _ to second division *(49)* _ _ _ _ _ _ _ Xerez in January 2009 and *(50)* _ _ August 6, 2009, Jozy Altidore joined Hull City FC (England) on a season-long loan with the option for Hull City to purchase his rights at the end of the 2009–10 season for a fee believed to be £6.5 million ($11 million).

Jozy Altidore
(Answer ID # 0694352)

1.	2.	3.
4.	5.	6.
7.	8.	9.
10.	11.	12.
13.	14.	15.
16.	17.	18.
19.	20.	21.
22.	23.	24.
25.	26.	27.
28.	29.	30.
31.	32.	33.
34.	35.	36.
37.	38.	39.
40.	41.	42.
43.	44.	45.

46.	47.	48.
49.	50.	

Answer Key 0492184
Word Bank

Altidore	S	eleven	program
Boca	Soccer	full	scored
Bradenton	States	goal	squad
Cup	U	himself	strikers
El	U-17	his	substitute
GBYSA	United	imposing	team
Haiti	World	in	the
Italy	a	member	was
Netherlands	against	of	were
November	and	-	on	with
On	as	one	won
Prep	coming	parents	
Qualifying	eighteenth	played	

Directions: Fill in each blank with a word from the word bank that best completes the story.

Jozy Altidore is *(1)* _____ of the powerful *(2)* _____ for the United *(3)* _____ national team. Born *(4)* _____ Livingston, New Jersey, *(5)* _____ was raised in *(6)* _____ Raton, Florida by *(7)* _____ Haitian parents. His *(8)* _____, Joseph and Giselle, *(9)* _____ both born in *(10)* _____ .

Jozy Altidore attended the *(11)* _____ Academy as a *(12)* _____ of the United States *(13)* _____ national team, and *(14)* _____ part of the *(15)* _____ at the 2005 FIFA U-17 *(16)* _____ Championship, appearing as *(17)* _____ substitute in the *(18)* _____ States' 3–1 win over *(19)* _____ and 2–0 loss to *(20)* _____ Netherlands. Before joining the *(21)* _____.S. U-17 Residency *(22)* _____ Altidore attended Boca *(23)* _____. Growing up, Altidore *(24)* _____ club soccer for *(25)* _____ and Boca Juniors *(26)* _____ Club.

Jozy Altidore played *(27)* _____ the 2010 FIFA World *(28)* _____ US Team as one *(29)* _____ four forwards. On *(30)* _____ 17, 2007, Jozy Altidore joined the *(31)* _____ United States national *(32)* _____ for a friendly *(33)* _____ South Africa just *(34)* _____ days after his *(35)* _____ birthday. The physically *(36)* _____ striker, Jozy Altidore, *(37)* _____ his first cap *(38)* _____ team USA in November 2007 *(39)* _____ has since moved *(40)* _____ into the reckoning *(41)* _____ a superb attacker. *(42)* _____ August 10, 2008, he scored against the *(43)* _____ to put the U.*(44)* _____. in front after *(45)* _____ on as a *(46)* _____. On March 28, 2009, Jozy Altidore *(47)* _____ his first away *(48)* _____ in World Cup *(49)* _____ in the 2–2 draw with *(50)* _____ Salvador. Although Jozy Altidore would find it difficult to secure significant playing time at the club level in Europe, his contributions to the US senior national team have been significant and consistent.

(Answer ID # 0492184)

1.	2.	3.
4.	5.	6.
7.	8.	9.
10.	11.	12.
13.	14.	15.
16.	17.	18.
19.	20.	21.
22.	23.	24.
25.	26.	27.
28.	29.	30.
31.	32.	33.
34.	35.	36.
37.	38.	39.
40.	41.	42.
43.	44.	45.
46.	47.	48.
49.	50.	

Lesson 23
Robbie Findley

Answer Key 0328095
Word Bank

April	Salt	conference)	national
Findley	State	earned	off
Galaxy's	USA's	for	put
Houston	West	form	remains
Klein	Year	fourth	run-up
LA	a	goals	scored
Lake	all	himself	settling
MLS	also	his	the
Nathan	an	in	traded
Oregon	and	leader	unlikely
Robbie	career	named	was

Directions: Fill in each blank with a word from the word bank that best completes the story.

Robbie Findley attended *(1)* _ _ _ _ _ _ State University. At Oregon *(2)* _ _ _ _ _ University Robbie Findley *(3)* _ _ _ _ _ _ _ All-Pacific-10 honors in *(4)* _ _ _ _ four seasons and *(5)* _ _ _ the Pac-10 (college athletic *(6)* _ _ _ _ _ _ _ _ _ _ _ Freshman of the *(7)* _ _ _ _ in 2003. He was *(8)* _ _ _ _ _ an NSCAA All-Far *(9)* _ _ _ _ selection three times, *(10)* _ _ _ finished his Oregon State *(11)* _ _ _ _ _ _ as the career *(12)* _ _ _ _ _ _ in game-winning goals and *(13)* _ _ _ _ ranking third in *(14)* _ _ _ _ _ _, third in points, and *(15)* _ _ _ _ _ _ _ in assists.

After *(16)* _ successful University career, *(17)* _ _ _ jet-heeled striker, Robbie *(18)* _ _ _ _ _ _ _, moved on to *(19)* _ _ _ _ _ lower leagues before *(20)* _ _ _ _ _ _ _ _ _ into MLS with *(21)* _ _ Galaxy in 2007. On *(22)* _ _ _ _ _ 8, 2007, Robbie Findley made *(23)* _ _ _ MLS debut in *(24)* _ _ _ _ _ _ _ _ season opener against the *(25)* _ _ _ _ _ _ _ _ Dynamo. Shortly after *(26)* _ _ _ _ _ _ Findley was sent *(27)* _ _ _ to Real Salt *(28)* _ _ _ _, where he still *(29)* _ _ _ _ _ _ _ today. Robbie Findley was *(30)* _ _ _ _ _ _ along with midfielder *(31)* _ _ _ _ _ _ Sturgis to Real *(32)* _ _ _ _ Lake in exchange *(33)* _ _ _ veteran forward Chris *(34)* _ _ _ _ _ on June 21, 2007. Robbie Findley *(35)* _ _ _ _ _ _ _ a raft of goals *(36)* _ _ Real Salt Lake's *(37)* _ _ _ _ _ _ _ _ run to the *(38)* _ _ _ crown in 2009, earning *(39)* _ _ _ _ _ _ _ a reputation as *(40)* _ _ "opportunistic predator." Robbie Findley's *(41)* _ _ _ _ for Real Salt Lake *(42)* _ _ him on the *(43)* _ _ _ _ _ _ _ _ team coach's radar in the *(44)* _ _ _ _ _ _ to South Africa

124

Robbie Findley
(Answer ID # 0328095)

1.	2.	3.
4.	5.	6.
7.	8.	9.
10.	11.	12.
13.	14.	15.
16.	17.	18.
19.	20.	21.
22.	23.	24.
25.	26.	27.
28.	29.	30.
31.	32.	33.
34.	35.	36.
37.	38.	39.
40.	41.	42.
43.	44.	

Africa	Tobago	call-up	national
American	United	camp	not
Coach	World	dual	off
Cup	against	eye	on
Findley	also	final	round
Findley's	ancestry	for	senior
June	and	had	settled
Robbie	attended	him	substitute
South	be	in	the
States	but	match	they
Switzerland	by	minutes	to

Directions: Fill in each blank with a word from the word bank that best completes the story.

Robbie Findley holds *(1)* _____ citizenship between USA *(2)* _____ Trinidad and Tobago *(3)* _____ he has chosen *(4)* _____ settle on the *(5)* _____ side of his *(6)* _____. In 2006, Robbie Findley *(7)* _____ a Trinidad and *(8)* _____ U-23 national team *(9)* _____ but he eventually *(10)* _____ with the US *(11)* _____ team. On October 9, 2007, *(12)* _____ Findley received a *(13)* _____ to the United *(14)* _____ senior national team *(15)* _____ its friendly against *(16)* _____, and entered the *(17)* _____ as a last-minute *(18)* _____.

Although he is usually *(19)* _____ a starter in *(20)* _____ US squad, Robbie *(21)* _____ good pace and *(22)* _____ for goal makes *(23)* _____ a good option *(24)* _____ the bench. Until *(25)* _____ Africa 2010 Robbie Findley *(26)* _____ only three caps for the *(27)* _____ Stars and Stripes. Robbie *(28)* _____ was selected by *(29)* _____ Bob Bradley to *(30)* _____ on the 23-man roster for the 2010 *(31)* _____ Cup in South *(32)* _____. He made his World *(33)* _____ debut against England *(34)* _____ June 12, 2010. On June 18, 2010 Robbie Findley *(35)* _____ played in the match *(36)* _____ Sloveniaon, and on *(37)* _____ 26, 2010 he also played 46 *(38)* _____ before being replaced *(39)* _____ Benny Feilhaber in the *(40)* _____ game for the *(41)* _____ States at 2010 World Cup *(42)* _____ South Africa when *(43)* _____ lost 1-2 in the *(44)* _____ of 16 against Ghana.

126

(Answer ID # 0973439)

1.	2.	3.
4.	5.	6.
7.	8.	9.
10.	11.	12.
13.	14.	15.
16.	17.	18.
19.	20.	21.
22.	23.	24.
25.	26.	27.
28.	29.	30.
31.	32.	33.
34.	35.	36.
37.	38.	39.
40.	41.	42.
43.	44.	

Lesson 24
US COACH Bob Bradley

Word Bank

Bob	Team	for	nine
Bradley	US	has	of
December	World	he	over
Essex	also	his	raised
Fire	appointment	in	round
MetroStars	be	is	team
Princeton	both	management	the
S	coach	manager	
South	colleges	managing	
States	expires	mater	

Directions: Fill in each blank with a word from the word bank that best completes the story.

Bob Bradley is *(1)* _____ coach who led *(2)* _____ USA to the *(3)* _____ of 16 in the 2010 *(4)* _____ Cup final in *(5)* _____ Africa. Bob Bradley *(6)* _____ served as the *(7)* _____ of the United *(8)* _____ men's national soccer *(9)* _____ since 2006. His contract *(10)* _____ in December 2010. It *(11)* _____ not certain if *(12)* _____ contract, to manage the *(13)* _____ national team would *(14)* _____ extended. Born and *(15)* _____ in New Jersey, *(16)* _____ Bradley attended West *(17)* _____ High School and *(18)* _____ University where he *(19)* _____ played soccer for *(20)* _____ school teams. Until his *(21)* _____ as the head *(22)* _____ of the US team *(23)* _____ served as coach *(24)* _____ several clubs and *(25)* _____, including his alma *(26)* _____, Princeton University. Bob *(27)* _____ was the first manager *(28)* _____ the expansion Chicago *(29)* _____. Before taking over the *(30)* _____ of the U.*(31)* _____ national team in *(32)* _____ 2006, Bob Bradley coached *(33)* _____ Major League Soccer, *(34)* _____ the Chicago Fire, *(35)* _____, and Chivas USA *(36)* _____ a span of *(37)* _____ seasons.

128

US COACH Bob Bradley
(Answer ID # 0461740)

1.	2.	3.
4.	5.	6.
7.	8.	9.
10.	11.	12.
13.	14.	15.
16.	17.	18.
19.	20.	21.
22.	23.	24.
25.	26.	27.
28.	29.	30.
31.	32.	33.
34.	35.	36.
37.		

Answer Key 0354581
Word Bank

After	New	born	newly
Arena	Soccer	coach	of
Bob	U	coached	off
Bradley	West	colleges	over
C	a	first	played
Chicago	again	for	school

D	alma	in	seasons
December	and	led	skills
In	appointment	manager	team
Jersey	assistant	managing	tender
League	at	mater	the
MetroStars	became	moving	to

Directions: Fill in each blank with a word from the word bank that best completes the story.

Bob Bradley was *(1)* _ _ _ _ and raised in *(2)* _ _ _ Jersey. He attended *(3)* _ _ _ _ _ Essex High School *(4)* _ _ _ Princeton University. He *(5)* _ _ _ _ _ _ soccer for both *(6)* _ _ _ _ _ _ teams. Until his *(7)* _ _ _ _ _ _ _ _ _ _ _ as the head *(8)* _ _ _ _ _ _ of the US *(9)* _ _ _ _ _ he served as coach *(10)* _ _ _ several clubs and *(11)* _ _ _ _ _ _ _ _ _, including his alma *(12)* _ _ _ _ _ _, Princeton University. Bob *(13)* _ _ _ _ _ _ _ _ took up his *(14)* _ _ _ _ _ managerial post as *(15)* _ _ _ _ _ _ _ _ _ coach to Bruce *(16)* _ _ _ _ _ _ at the University *(17)* _ _ Ohio at the *(18)* _ _ _ _ _ _ _ age of 22, before *(19)* _ _ _ _ _ _ _ on to his *(20)* _ _ _ _ mater Princeton in New *(21)* _ _ _ _ _ _ as head coach. *(22)* _ _ his eleven seasons *(23)* _ _ Princeton University (1984 to 1995), *(24)* _ _ _ _ Bradley sharpened his *(25)* _ _ _ _ _ _ as coach. Bob Bradley *(26)* _ _ _ the Tigers from 1984 *(27)* _ _ 1995, winning two Ivy *(28)* _ _ _ _ _ _ _ titles and reaching *(29)* _ _ _ NCAA Final Four *(30)* _ _ 1993. He then headed *(31)* _ _ _ after Major League *(32)* _ _ _ _ _ _ _ for greener pastures in 1996. Bob Bradley *(33)* _ _ _ _ _ _ _ Arena's assistant once *(34)* _ _ _ _ _ _ with one of the *(35)* _ _ _ _ _ _ formed Major League Soccer team, *(36)* _.C. United in 1996. *(37)* _ _ _ _ _ _ two seasons with D.*(38)* _. United, Bob Bradley became the first *(39)* _ _ _ _ _ _ _ _ of the expansion *(40)* _ _ _ _ _ _ _ _ Fire. Before taking *(41)* _ _ _ _ _ the management of the *(42)* _.S national team in *(43)* _ _ _ _ _ _ _ _ _ 2006, Bob Bradley had *(44)* _ _ _ _ _ _ _ _ Major League Soccer, *(45)* _ _ _ _ _ _ _ _ _ the Chicago Fire, *(46)* _ _ _ _ _ _ _ _ _ _ _ _, and Chivas USA over *(47)* _ span of nine *(48)* _ _ _ _ _ _ _.

(Answer ID # 0354581)

1.	2.	3.
4.	5.	6.
7.	8.	9.
10.	11.	12.
13.	14.	15.

16.	17.	18.
19.	20.	21.
22.	23.	24.
25.	26.	27.
28.	29.	30.
31.	32.	33.
34.	35.	36.
37.	38.	39.
40.	41.	42.
43.	44.	45.
46.	47.	48.

Answer Key 0604388
Word Bank
CLUB ACHIEVEMENTS

After	assistant	manager	the
Bob	double	named	their
Bradley	exit	old	this
Bruce	final	post	titles
Cup	first	professional	to
Fire	fixtures	prospects	up
League's	franchise	resigned	was
MetroStars	hard-luck	season	went
Open	he	seasons	win
Red	in	short	with
United	including	struggling	would

| Year-1998 | left | success |
| and | make | suffering |

CLUB ACHIEVEMENTS

Directions: Fill in each blank with a word from the word bank that best completes the story.

In his US Major *(1)* _ _ _ _ _ _ _ _ inaugural season, Bob *(2)* _ _ _ _ _ _ _ settled in as *(3)* _ _ _ _ _ _ _ _ _ _ coach to his *(4)* _ _ _ friend and mentor *(5)* _ _ _ _ _ _ Arena at DC *(6)* _ _ _ _ _ _ _, where he helped *(7)* _ _ _ side to back-to-back *(8)* _ _ _ _ _ _ _ in 1996 and 1997. Bradley's *(9)* _ _ _ _ _ appearance as a *(10)* _ _ _ _ _ _ _ _ _ _ _ _ _ head coach was *(11)* _ _ Chicago, Illinois, where *(12)* _ _ had an unqualified *(13)* _ _ _ _ _ _ _ with the Illinois *(14)* _ _ _ _ _ _ _ _ _ _. He helped Chicago *(15)* _ _ the double header in *(16)* _ _ _ _ _ first year, picking *(17)* _ _ the MLS crown *(18)* _ _ _ winning the US *(19)* _ _ Cup in 1998.

As coach, *(20)* _ _ _ Bradley led Chicago *(21)* _ _ _ _ to the MLS *(22)* _ _ _ _ and US Open Cup *(23)* _ _ _ _ _ _ in 1998, and for *(24)* _ _ _ _ _ success, he was *(25)* _ _ _ _ _ _ MLS Coach of the *(26)* _ _ _ _ _ _ _ _ _ _. He led Chicago Fire to *(27)* _ _ _ _ more silverware in 2000 *(28)* _ _ _ _ _ _ _ _ _ _ _ the US Open Cup. *(29)* _ _ _ _ _ _ the 2002 MLS season, he *(30)* _ _ _ _ _ _ _ _ _ as manager of the Fire and *(31)* _ _ _ _ _ to manage his *(32)* _ _ _ _ _ _ _ _ _ _ _ home state team, the *(33)* _ _ _ _ _ _ _ _ _ _ _ _ (now the New York *(34)* _ _ _ Bulls) where he *(35)* _ _ _ _ _ _ spend only two *(36)* _ _ _ _ _ _ _ _. He soon led the *(37)* _ _ _ _ _ _ _ _ _ _ Red Bulls side to their first Open Cup *(38)* _ _ _ _ _; however, this was *(39)* _ _ _ _ _ lived. In October 2005, *(40)* _ _ _ _ only three games *(41)* _ _ _ _ in the regular *(42)* _ _ _ _ _ _ _, Red Bulls' was struggling to *(43)* _ _ _ _ the playoff. All *(44)* _ _ _ _ _ _ _ _ _ _ had reduced after *(45)* _ _ _ _ _ _ _ _ _ _ losses in back-to-back *(46)* _ _ _ _ _ _ _ _ _. At this time Bob Bradley *(47)* _ _ _ relieved from his *(48)* _ _ _ _ as coach. After his *(49)* _ _ _ _ from MetroStars in 2005, Bob Bradley was named the *(50)* _ _ _ _ _ _ _ of Chivas USA, the Los Angeles club in 2006 after a dismal opening season. He managed to lead Chivas USA to a third-place finish in the Western Conference from behind.

CLUB ACHIEVEMENTS
(Answer ID # 0604388)

1.	2.	3.
4.	5.	6.
7.	8.	9.

10. _____	11. _____	12. _____
13. _____	14. _____	15. _____
16. _____	17. _____	18. _____
19. _____	20. _____	21. _____
22. _____	23. _____	24. _____
25. _____	26. _____	27. _____
28. _____	29. _____	30. _____
31. _____	32. _____	33. _____
34. _____	35. _____	36. _____
37. _____	38. _____	39. _____
40. _____	41. _____	42. _____
43. _____	44. _____	45. _____
46. _____	47. _____	48. _____
49. _____	50. _____	

US NATIONAL TEAM ACCOMPLISHMENTS
Answer Key 0360112
Word Bank

Bob	also	he	straight
Bruce	appointed	his	team
CONCACAF	be	home-grown	that
Cup	beating	immediate	the
December	being	in	thrilling

He	big-name	men's	to
Reyna	but	men's	up
S	coaching	mind	was
US	crop	officially	which
United	cultivate	old	whose
University	decision	on	youngsters
World	failures	over	
a	had	series	

Directions: Fill in each blank with a word from the word bank that best completes the story.

US NATIONAL TEAM ACCOMPLISHMENTS

His friend, Bruce Arena *(1)* _____ the U.S. *(2)* _____ national team's manager *(3)* _____ took Team USA *(4)* _____ the 2006 FIFA World *(5)* _____ in Germany where *(6)* _____ got eliminated at *(7)* _____ group stage. Initially the *(8)* _____ States Soccer Federation *(9)* _____ promised a foreign, *(10)* _____ coach to follow *(11)* _____ Bruce Arena after the *(12)* _____ of the 2006 FIFA *(13)* _____ Cup in Germany, *(14)* _____ they changed their *(15)* _____ to stick with *(16)* _____ local manager. The *(17)* _____ to opt for *(18)* _____ coach fell on *(19)* _____ Bradley. He was *(20)* _____ the interim U.*(21)* _____. coach in 2006 and *(22)* _____ soon proved to *(23)* _____ the thoughtful tactician *(24)* _____ approach would reap *(25)* _____ benefits for the US *(26)* _____ soccer team. He *(27)* _____ took over from *(28)* _____ friend and mentor *(29)* _____ Arena as manager *(30)* _____ May 15, 2007 after a *(31)* _____ of successful friendlies *(32)* _____ included a 2–0 win *(33)* _____ Mexico. Bob Bradley *(34)* _____ led the USA to *(35)* _____ Gold Cup glory *(36)* _____ the summer of 2007, *(37)* _____ Mexico in a *(38)* _____ final in Chicago.

After *(39)* _____ named head coach in *(40)* _____ 2008, Bradley set about *(41)* _____ away to build a *(42)* _____, using his experience *(43)* _____ youth players, at *(44)* _____ and Olympic level, to *(45)* _____ a team of *(46)* _____ looking beyond the *(47)* _____ idols like Claudio *(48)* _____ and Brian McBride. *(49)* _____ brought in a *(50)* _____ of new players like his son Michael Bradley, Sacha Kljestan, Jozy Altidore and immediately made an impact in the US national team. The initial results were convincing.

134

US NATIONAL TEAM ACCOMPLISHMENTS
(Answer ID # 0360112)

1.	2.	3.
4.	5.	6.
7.	8.	9.
10.	11.	12.
13.	14.	15.
16.	17.	18.
19.	20.	21.
22.	23.	24.
25.	26.	27.
28.	29.	30.
31.	32.	33.
34.	35.	36.
37.	38.	39.
40.	41.	42.
43.	44.	45.
46.	47.	48.
49.	50.	

Answer Key 0177749
Word Bank

Bob	South	first-place	records
Bradley	U	for	shock
Central	US	in	the
Confederations	World	lead	then
Cup	a	led	this
Egypt	after	losing	victory
FIFA	away	loss	win
Ghana	champions	qualification	world
Gold	coach	qualifying	year
October	defeat	ranked	
S	end	reach	

Directions: Fill in each blank with a word from the word bank that best completes the story.

In summer of 2007 *(1) AHCOC* _____ Bob Bradley led *(2) EHT* _____ United States to the 2007 *(3) LGDO* _____ Cup Final, where the *(4) US* _____ beat rivals Mexico 2–1 *(5) ROF* _____ the second time *(6) IN* _____ four months. Coach *(7) ADBLREY* _____ lost his first *(8) AYWA* _____ game to Argentina in the 2007 Gold *(9) UCP* _____ opener 4–1, though but *(10) IHTS* _____ was his first *(11) DEEAFT* _____ and the first US *(12) SLSO* _____ in over a *(13) YRAE* _____ since losing to *(14) AHGNA* _____ (1-2) in the 2006 World Cup.

In 2009 *(15) BBO* _____ Bradley orchestrated a *(16) OCKHS* _____ heard around the *(17) LDOWR* _____ with wins over *(18) EYTGP* _____ and Spain to *(19) ECHRA* _____ the final of the *(20) IFAF* _____ Confederations Cup, eventually *(21) LSGION* _____ out to Brazil *(22) FRTAE* _____ taking a 2-0 first-half *(23) AELD* _____.

As coach, Bradley led the *(24) U* _____.S. team to *(25) A* _____ 2nd place finish in the 2009 *(26) FIOSEONDATECNR* _____ Cup, including a 2–0 *(27) YRVOITC* _____ over Spain, the *(28) HTEN* _____ world's number one *(29) ARDNEK* _____ team and European *(30) MHPAIOSCN* _____. This victory would *(31) EDN* _____ Spain's 35 game unbeaten *(32) DROECSR* _____. He led the U.*(33) S* _____ national team to *(34) NAUICLAIFOITQ* _____ for the 2010 World Cup in *(35) THSUO* _____ Africa, with a 3-2 away *(36) IWN* _____ against Honduras on *(37) OROCETB* _____ 10. Bob Bradley also *(38) ELD* _____ the USA to a *(39) EPTCF-RSALI* _____ finish in North, *(40) LNERTAC* _____ American and Caribbean *(41) FUIAYNQGIL* _____ for the 2010 FIFA *(42) WLODR* _____ Cup.

136

(Answer ID # 0177749)

1.	2.	3.
4.	5.	6.
7.	8.	9.
10.	11.	12.
13.	14.	15.
16.	17.	18.
19.	20.	21.
22.	23.	24.
25.	26.	27.
28.	29.	30.
31.	32.	33.
34.	35.	36.
37.	38.	39.
40.	41.	42.

Answer Key 0948938
Word Bank

B	While	did	never
Brazil	World	done	past
C	a	far	reaching
Cup	after	for	second
England	and	high-power	team
He	another	in	the
I	at	its	to
South	bring	just	topped
USA	coach	led	yet

Directions: Fill in each blank with a word from the word bank that best completes the story.

Bob Bradley At South Africa 2010

Bob Bradley's feat at *(1) HSTUO* _____ Africa 2010 FIFA World *(2) CPU* _____ is impressive, having *(3) PPEDOT* _____ their group C *(4) AT* _____ the end of *(5) TEH* _____ group stage. He *(6) LDE* _____ the US national *(7) TMAE* _____ to top group *(8) C* _____ by drawing 1-1 with *(9) NLGENDA* _____ and 2-2 with Slovenia *(10) DNA* _____ beating Algeria 1-0. Unfortunately, *(11) ASU* _____ later lost in *(12) IST* _____ first match of the *(13) NCOSDE* _____ round to Ghana 2-1, *(14) ETFRA* _____ extra time.

As a *(15) CHOCA* _____, Bob Bradley has *(16) REEVN* _____ played professional soccer. *(17) HE* _____ has, however, played *(18) A* _____ proud four years at *(19) RE-WGIOHHP* _____ Princeton University between 1976 and 1980. *(20) LEWIH* _____ some think he *(21) IDD* _____ not do enough *(22) TO* _____ carry Team USA *(23) ATPS* _____ round of 16 in the *(24) JTSU* _____ ended FIFA World Cup, *(25) I* _____ think B has *(26) ONED* _____ a great job to *(27) BGRIN* _____ the team this *(28) AFR* _____. His record speaks *(29) FRO* _____ itself. When giving *(30) TNRHEOA* _____ chance I believe *(31) B* _____ will do great *(32) IN* _____ FIFA World Cup 2014 in *(33) LARBIZ* _____. Team USA is *(34) TEY* _____ to repeat her 1930 *(35) LWRDO* _____ Cup success of *(36) EGIRACHN* _____ the semi-final.

138

Bob Bradley At South Africa 2010
(Answer ID # 0948938)

1.	2.	3.
4.	5.	6.
7.	8.	9.
10.	11.	12.
13.	14.	15.
16.	17.	18.
19.	20.	21.
22.	23.	24.
25.	26.	27.
28.	29.	30.
31.	32.	33.
34.	35.	36.

SECTION 3 (MCQs)

Lesson 25
TEAM USA SOUTH AFRICA 2010 FIFA WORLD CUP SQUAD
Answer Key 0625398

Word List

Benny FEILHABER	Edson BUDDLE	Jonathan SPECTOR	Oguchi ONYEWU
Brad GUZAN	Francisco TORRES	Jozy ALTIDORE	Ricardo CLARK
Clarence GOODSON	Herculez GOMEZ	Landon DONOVAN	Robbie FINDLEY
Clint DEMPSEY	Jay DeMERIT	Maurice EDU	Steve
DaMarcus BEASLEY	Jonathan BORNSTEIN	Michael BRADLEY	CHERUNDOLO
			Stuart HOLDEN

Matching

Match each definition with a word.

1. **a.** He is a big, strong central defender with the US national team. He is an American soccer player, who played as a defender for IK Start in Norway.

   b. He attended Annandale High School his freshman and sophomore seasons before moving to W.T. Woodson High School.

   Clarence GOODSON

2. **a.** He is the second American to score goals in two different FIFA World Cup finals tournaments, in 2006 and 2010.

   b. He is an American soccer player who played for the United States national team and English Premier League club Fulham.

   _____

3. **a.** 2. He was an U.S. soccer player who played defence for Chivas USA of Major League Soccer and for the United States national team.

   b. He was a relatively new member of the US national team during South Africa 2010 FIFA World Cup.

   _____

4. **a.** His only goal at South Africa 2010 FIFA World Cup was denied. He wept when Ghana scored against the US (2-1) to deny US the chance to go past round 16 in the South Africa 2010 FIFA World Cup.

   b. He cut short his time at university to join Major League Soccer. In 2007 He was drafted by Toronto FC as the first overall pick of the 2007 MLS SuperDraft.

   _____

5. **a.** He was born in Aberdeen, Scotland and grew up in Sugar Land, Texas, after moving there with his family when he was only 10.

b. He stayed a year with English club Sunderland and left to the United States to play in Major League Soccer (MLS) with hometown club Houston Dynamo for the 2006 season.

_____

6. **a.** In 1999 He picked up the Golden Ball as the best player at the FIFA U-17 World Championship in New Zealand and soon afterwards earned his first call-up to a United States national team training camp.

b. As his club's captain, He led the Galaxy to MLS Cup 2009, which they lost on penalties.

_____

7. **a.** He is an American soccer player who played for the United States soccer team. He is nicknamed 'Jitterbug' for his deft tricks and jinking moves with the ball at his feet.

b. He earned a place with the U.S. squad that finished in the quarterfinals of the 2002 FIFA World Cup, where he played in all three group stage matches

.

_____

8. **a.** On May 11, 2010, He was named to the U.S. national team's provisional 30-man World Cup roster.

b. He played his youth soccer at the Chicago Magic Soccer Club, and for the varsity soccer team at Providence Catholic High School in Illinois, from which he graduated in 2003; he then went on to play two seasons of college soccer at the University of South Carolina (USC).

_____

9. **a.** He was named an NSCAA All-Far West selection three times, and finished his Oregon State career as the career leader in game-winning goals and also ranking third in goals, third in points, and fourth in assists.

b. On April 8, 2007, he made his MLS debut in Galaxy's season opener against the Houston   Dynamo.

_____

10. **a.** 2. He graduated from the United States Soccer Federation's Bradenton Academy in 2003.

b. He made his first USA senior national appearance in 2003 against Jamaica.

_____

11. **a.** Born in the state of Texas, he is the son of mixed Mexican and American parentage. **b.** He is an American soccer player who played as a midfielder for Pachuca in the Primera División de México and the United States national team. _____	12. **a.** He is an American soccer player who also played for Eintracht Frankfurt in the Fußball-Bundesliga. **b.** He got his first senior cap on October 12, 2005 against Panama, and scored his first international goal on July 2, 2007 against Paraguay in the 2007 Copa America _____
13. **a.** He began his club career in the US lower leagues; he made the move to MLS in 2001 with Columbus Crew, where he scored an impressive 42 goals in 101 appearances for the Ohio club. **b.** He began his professional career in 2000, when he signed with the Long Island Rough Riders of the A-League _____	14. **a.** As part of the US squad for South Africa 2010 FIFA World Cup he was coached by his father Bob Bradley. **b.** He is an American soccer player who played as a midfielder for Borussia Mönchengladbach of the German Fußball-Bundesliga and the United States national team. _____
15. **a.** He is an American soccer player of Nigerian descent. He also holds Belgian citizenship. He speaks English and fluent French. As at South Africa 2010, he was the tallest outfield player in U.S. team history; two goalkeepers have been taller though. **b.** He played two years of college soccer at Clemson University, and moved to Europe in 2002, signing with Metz of Ligue 1 in France. _____	16. **a.** He scored the game-winning goal in the 2005 Lamar Hunt U.S. Open Cup Final, then helped the Galaxy to a rare Cup 'double' when they also won the 2005 MLS Cup. **b.** He is an American soccer player who played for Pachuca in the Primera División de México and brother of Mixed martial arts (MMA) fighter Ulysses Gomez, a Mexican-American professional who competes in the flyweight and bantamweight divisions. _____

| 17. **a.** He grew up in San Diego and attended Mt. Carmel High School in Rancho Penasquitos. Before joining Hannover 96, he played two years of college soccer at the University of Portland, from 1997 to 1998.

b. He is a native of California who helps to make a strong rearguard for Team USA.

———————— | 18. **a.** He is of Austrian-Jewish ancestry who was born in Rio de Janeiro. Benny Feilhaber's paternal grandfather emigrated from Austria to Brazil in 1938 to escape the Nazi regime.

b. He played college soccer at the University of California, Los Angeles (UCLA), where he became a mainstay in the Bruins' midfield.

———————— |
| 19. **a.** Growing up, he played club soccer for GBYSA and Boca Juniors Soccer Club. His parents, Joseph and Giselle, were both born in Haiti

b. He is a powerful striker for the United States national team who also played club soccer for GBYSA and Boca Juniors Soccer Club.

———————— | 20. **a.** He is an American soccer player who played for and captained Watford F.C. at one point in time.

b. Following his two week trial at Northwood in July 2004, he signed a one year contract with Watford to play in their 2004–05 season and has since been a regular in the Watford lineup until 2010, when he was released from his contract

———————— |

Lesson 25B
TEAM USA SOUTH AFRICA 2010 FIFA WORLD CUP SQUAD
Answer Key 0895469

Select the definition that most nearly defines the given word.

21. **Clarence GOODSON**
    Ⓐ A big, strong central defender with the US national team; he is an American soccer player, who played as a defender for IK Start in Norway.
    Ⓑ He is an American soccer player who played as a midfielder for Borussia Mönchengladbach of the German Fußball-Bundesliga and the United States national team.
    Ⓒ He played for the La Jolla Nomads club team which won the California State Championship six times with him on the roster as a youth before entering

22. **Edson BUDDLE**
    Ⓐ He first began kicking a ball around with the Latin America immigrant population in the small Texas town of Nacogdoches, where he grew up humbly in a trailer. As a versatile attacking player, he could be used on either wing or as a striker.
    Ⓑ He is an American soccer player who played for Los Angeles Galaxy in Major League Soccer and the United States national team.
    Ⓒ He earned his first international start on March 28, 2007, during a friendly against Guatemala.

23. **Robbie FINDLEY**
    Ⓐ He was named an NSCAA All-Far West selection three times, and finished his Oregon State career as the career leader in game-winning goals and also ranking third in goals, third in points, and fourth in assists.
    Ⓑ On May 11, 2010, he was named to the U.S. national team's provisional 30-man World Cup roster.
    Ⓒ On December 1, 2006, he was traded to the Colorado Rapids along with Ugo Ihemelu in exchange for Joe Cannon.

24. **Stuart HOLDEN**
    Ⓐ After practicing with them for several weeks, Stuart Holden officially joined Premier League side Bolton Wanderers on January 25, 2010.
    Ⓑ Following his two week trial at Northwood in July 2004, he signed a one year contract with Watford to play in their 2004–05 season and has since been a regular in the Watford lineup until 2010, when he was released from his contract
    Ⓒ As his club's captain, he led the Galaxy to MLS Cup 2009, which they lost on penalties.

144

25. Clint DEMPSEY
- (A) On May 5, 2007, Clint Dempsey scored his first and only goal of the 2006–07 season for Fulham after coming on as a 54th minute substitute against Liverpool, in a vital match which Fulham won 1–0. The goal ensured Fulham's top flight status for the 2007–08 season
- (B) He is an American soccer player who also played for Eintracht Frankfurt in the Fußball-Bundesliga.
- (C) As part of the US squad for South Africa 2010 FIFA World Cup he was coached by his father Bob Bradley.

26. Steve CHERUNDOLO
- (A) He played for the La Jolla Nomads club team which won the California State Championship six times with him on the roster as a youth before entering
- (B) He is a powerful striker for the United States national team who also played club soccer for GBYSA and Boca Juniors Soccer Club.
- (C) He is of Austrian-Jewish ancestry who was born in Rio de Janeiro. Benny Feilhaber's paternal grandfather emigrated from Austria to Brazil in 1938 to escape the Nazi regime.

27. Oguchi ONYEWU
- (A) 4. He attended Los Alamitos High School where he played soccer for all four years.
- (B) His only World Cup goal was disallowed on June 18, 2010 against Slovenia; in the 85th minute with the game delicately poised at 2–2, he volleyed in a free kick from Landon Donovan straight into the net but referee Koman Coulibaly disallowed the goal for no apparent reason.
- (C) He played two years of college soccer at Clemson University, and moved to Europe in 2002, signing with Metz of Ligue 1 in France.

28. Landon DONOVAN
- (A) After practicing with them for several weeks, he officially joined Premier League side Bolton Wanderers on January 25, 2010.
- (B) He is an American soccer player of Nigerian descent. Oguchi Onyewu also holds Belgian citizenship. He speaks English and fluent French. As at South Africa 2010, the tallest outfield player in U.S. team history; two goalkeepers have been taller though.
- (C) In November 2008 he trained with FC Bayern Munich, and later joined the German club on loan until the start of the 2009 MLS season in mid-March.

29. Jonathan BORNSTEIN
- (A) 2. He was an U.S. soccer player who played defence for Chivas USA of Major League Soccer and for the United States national team.
- (B) He signed for the MetroStars (now the New York Red Bulls in 2006 and made his professional debut on August 23, 2006, as a substitute in a 3–1 U.S. Open Cup loss to D.C. United.
- (C) He played college soccer at the University of Illinois at Chicago, where he moved from playing forward to defender.

30. Jozy ALTIDORE
- (A) He signed for the MetroStars (now the New York Red Bulls in 2006 and made his professional debut on August 23, 2006, as a substitute in a 3–1 U.S. Open Cup loss to D.C. United.
- (B) 2. He graduated from the United States Soccer Federation's Bradenton Academy in 2003.
- (C) He was born in Aberdeen, Scotland and grew up in Sugar Land, Texas, after moving there with his family when he was only 10.

31. Ricardo CLARK

(A) It was with the Dynamo in Texas that he began to really stand out in the holding midfield role, winning back-to-back MLS titles in 2006 and 2007.

(B) He is an American soccer player who played for the United States national team and Real Salt Lake in Major League Soccer.

(C) He is an American soccer player who played as a midfielder for Pachuca in the Primera División de México and the United States national team.

32. Jay DeMERIT

(A) On September 3, 2008, he was traded to Kansas City Wizards in exchange for allocation money, a fourth round 2009 MLS SuperDraft pick and a first round 2009 MLS Supplemental Draft pick.

(B) Growing up, he played club soccer for GBYSA and Boca Juniors Soccer Club. His parents, Joseph and Giselle, were both born in Haiti

(C) He is an American soccer player who played for and captained Watford F.C. at one point in time.

33. Herculez GOMEZ

He attended the Bradenton Academy as a member of the United States U-17 national team, and was part of the squad at the 2005 FIFA U-17 World Championship, appearing as a substitute in the United States' 3–1 win over Italy and 2–0 loss to the Netherlands

(B) He is an American soccer player who played for Pachuca in the Primera División de México and brother of Mixed martial arts (MMA) fighter Ulysses Gomez, a Mexican-American professional who competes in the flyweight and bantamweight divisions.

(C) He played one year of college soccer at State Fair Community College, leading them to the 1999 NJCAA Division I National Championship.

34. Brad GUZAN

(A) He played his youth soccer at the Chicago Magic Soccer Club, and for the varsity soccer team at Providence Catholic High School in Illinois, from which he graduated in 2003; he then went on to play two seasons of college soccer at the University of South Carolina (USC).

(B) He scored the game-winning goal in the 2005 Lamar Hunt U.S. Open Cup Final, then helped the Galaxy to a rare Cup 'double' when they also won the 2005 MLS Cup.

(C) He was a relatively new member of the US national team during South Africa 2010 FIFA World Cup.

35. Benny FEILHABER
- (A) He is an American soccer midfielder, who played for AGF Aarhus in the Danish First Division and the United States national team.
- (B) He began his professional career in 2000, when he signed with the Long Island Rough Riders of the A-League
- (C) After becoming a regular member of the New York Red Bulls squad he was transferred to the San Jose Earthquakes in 2005 and he then moved again - with the rest of the team in a location change to Houston, where they became the Dynamo - in 2006.

36. Maurice EDU
- (A) His only goal at South Africa 2010 FIFA World Cup was denied. He wept when Ghana scored against the US (2-1) to deny US the chance to go past round 16 in the South Africa 2010 FIFA World Cup.
- (B) He was eligible to play for either USA or Mexico, but he turned down the opportunity to play with the Americans at the 2008 Beijing Olympic Games.
- (C) He attended Annandale High School his freshman and sophomore seasons before moving to W.T. Woodson High School.

37. Jonathan SPECTOR
- (A) He is a native of California who helps to make a strong rearguard for Team USA.
- (B) He stayed a year with English club Sunderland and left to the United States to play in Major League Soccer (MLS) with hometown club Houston Dynamo for the 2006 season.
- (C) 6. He played high school football at St. Viator High School and started his club football career with Schwaben AC in Buffalo Grove, Illinois, before joining national power Chicago Sockers.

38. Francisco TORRES
- He made his international debut in a friendly against Sweden on January 19, 2008.
- (B) He got his first senior cap on October 12, 2005 against Panama, and scored his first international goal on July 2, 2007 against Paraguay in the 2007 Copa America
- (C) Born in the state of Texas, he is the son of mixed Mexican and American parentage.

39. DaMarcus BEASLEY
- (A) He is a Scottish-born American footballer who played for Bolton Wanderers in the English Premier League.
- (B) He earned a place with the U.S. squad that finished in the quarterfinals of the 2002 FIFA World Cup, where he played in all three group stage matches.
- (C) He grew up in San Diego and attended Mt. Carmel High School in Rancho Penasquitos. Before joining

40. Michael BRADLEY
- (A) He played college soccer at the University of California, Los Angeles (UCLA), where he became a mainstay in the Bruins' midfield.
- (B) As part of the US squad for South Africa 2010 FIFA World Cup he was coached by his father Bob Bradley.
- (C) On April 8, 2007, he made his MLS debut in Galaxy's season opener against the Houston Dynamo.

| Hannover 96, Cherundolo played two years of college soccer at the University of Portland, from 1997 to 1998. | |

Chapter 26
History of SOCCER IN USA

History

Name

Answer Key

Date

0443616

Complete each sentence using the words in the word list.

Consolidated	Impressive	Folded	to
Tournament	Relegated	for	

_____1. U.S. opened the 1994 FIFA World Cup ____ with a 1–1 draw against Switzerland in the Pontiac Silverdome in the suburbs of Detroit.

_____2. Many forms of the kicking games were used to forward the ball to the goal line until American teams began to use the ____ London 1863 Football Association rules

_____3. 1998 FIFA World Cup was held in France from 10 June ____ 12 July 1998. Unfortunately US could not sustain her former feat. Team USA finished in last place in its group and 32nd in the field of 32 in France.

_____4. By the end of 1984, the North American Soccer League (NASL) had ____ and there was no senior outdoor soccer league operating in the United States. As a result, many top American players, moved overseas, primarily to Europe.

_____5. To provide a more stable national team program and renew interest in the NASL, U.S. Soccer entered the national team into the league ____ the 1983 season as Team America but many players rather preferred to play for their clubs rather than for Team America. Hence Team America lacked the continuity

_____6. Despite the United States' relative success in men's soccer in the 1930s and 1950, by 1970 men's soccer had been ____ to the shadows; the seriousness and potency of US Men Soccer Team was gone.

_____7. The team lost all three group matches, 0–2 ____ Germany, 1–2 to Iran, and 0–1 to Yugoslavia in 1998.

_____8. United States has made nine appearances out of the total of nineteen FIFA World Cup events to date (As of April 2011). Comparatively United States has a record of many ____ World Cup victories than many so called soccer nations around the globe.

Pioneers	Headline	remain	Podium	Global

_____ 9. FIFA was birthed in 1904 and the first FIFA World Cup was held in 1930. United States is one of the ____ to play soccer as a national sport. Back in the early 18th century

_____ 10. In the 1930 FIFA World Cup, Team USA finished on the ____ behind Uruguay, the eventual champions and Brazil, runner up

_____ 11. When the FIFA World Cup was first held in Uruguay in 1930, United States was one of the favorites beside Brazil, Argentina and Uruguay. These were also the few major soccer teams (or nations) outside of Europe who would contest in the ____ competition.

_____ 12. Men's soccer would ____ a recess sport in the U.S. for many years from 1951 to 1970.

_____ 13. It all began in 1989 when FIFA named the United States as the host nation for 1994 FIFA World Cup. All of a sudden America's attention was drawn to soccer. The game which had now become irrelevant, all of a sudden became the ____ news.

_____ 14. FIFA was birthed in 1904 and the first FIFA World Cup was held in 1930. United States is one of the **(Relegated, pioneers, Folded)** to play soccer as a national sport. Back in the early 18th century

_____ 15. When the FIFA World Cup was first held in Uruguay in 1930, United States was one of the favorites beside Brazil, Argentina and Uruguay. These were also the few major soccer teams (or nations) outside of Europe who would contest in the **(global, Folded, Pioneers)** competition.

_____ 16. The team lost all three group matches, 0–2 **(Pioneers, To, Impressive)** Germany, 1–2 to Iran, and 0–1 to Yugoslavia in 1998.

_____ 17. United States has made nine appearances out of the total of nineteen FIFA World Cup events to date (As of April 2011). Comparatively United States has a record of many **(Consolidated, impressive, Podium)** World Cup victories than many so called soccer nations around the globe.

_____ 18. To provide a more stable national team program and renew interest in the NASL, U.S. Soccer entered the national team into the league **(Global, For, Tournament)** the 1983 season as Team America but many players rather preferred to play for their clubs rather than for Team America. Hence Team America lacked the continuity

19. Many forms of the kicking games were used to forward the ball to the goal line until American teams began to use the **(Impressive, consolidated, Relegated)** London 1863 Football Association rules

20. It all began in 1989 when FIFA named the United States as the host nation for 1994 FIFA World Cup. All of a sudden America's attention was drawn to soccer. The game which had now become irrelevant, all of a sudden became the **(headline, Pioneers, Tournament)** news.

21. In the 1930 FIFA World Cup, Team USA finished on the **(podium, Relegated, Consolidated)** behind Uruguay, the eventual champions and Brazil, runner up

22. Despite the United States' relative success in men's soccer in the 1930s and 1950, by 1970 men's soccer had been **(Global, Folded, relegated)** to the shadows; the seriousness and potency of US Men Soccer Team was gone.

SECTION 4 SPORTS ANALOGIES

Lesson 27
Answer Key 03176851

Study the relationship between the first set of words. Pick the word that completes the second pair with this same relationship.

1.	arrowhead	:	_____	::	wigwam	:	home
	Ⓐ camouflage	Ⓑ weapon		Ⓒ soldier		Ⓓ uniform	

2.	transgressions	:	offenses	::	atonement	:	_____
	Ⓐ penance	Ⓑ disgrace		Ⓒ lying		Ⓓ ignorance	

3.	defense	:	block	::	_____	:	field goal
	Ⓐ umpire	Ⓑ team		Ⓒ coach		Ⓓ offense	

4.	ambitions	:	goals	::	repercussions	:	_____
	Ⓐ opposition	Ⓑ questions		Ⓒ consequences	Ⓓ accidents		

5.	conquer	:	defeat	::	rebellion	:	_____
	Ⓐ treaty	Ⓑ triumph		Ⓒ defend		Ⓓ revolt	

6.	home	:	burglar	::	ship	:	_____
	Ⓐ explore	Ⓑ pirate		Ⓒ ocean		Ⓓ cannon	

7.	antagonize	:	oppose	::	eschew	:	_____
	Ⓐ avoid	Ⓑ confuse		Ⓒ request		Ⓓ entice	

8.	induce	:	cause	::	allay	:	_____
	Ⓐ defend	Ⓑ search		Ⓒ relieve		Ⓓ reduce	

9.	winter	:	hockey	::	spring	:	_____
	Ⓐ football	Ⓑ diving		Ⓒ ice skating	Ⓓ baseball		

10.	Canadian Indians	:	lacrosse	::	Mexican Indians	:	_____
	Ⓐ tennis	Ⓑ handball		Ⓒ football		Ⓓ baseball	

11.	brown	:	football	::	black and white	:	_____
	Ⓐ soccer ball	Ⓑ baseball		Ⓒ basketball	Ⓓ tennis ball		

12.	soccer	:	_____	::	basketball	:	hoop
	Ⓐ idea	Ⓑ plan		Ⓒ goal		Ⓓ weapon	

13. class : teacher :: team : _____

Ⓐ sports Ⓑ coach Ⓒ uniform Ⓓ ball

14. soccer : field :: swimming : _____

Ⓐ bowling alley Ⓑ ocean Ⓒ ice rink Ⓓ sand

15. soccer : goal :: football : _____

Ⓐ hole-in-one Ⓑ strike Ⓒ touchdown Ⓓ home run

16. court : basketball :: field : _____

Ⓐ swimming Ⓑ soccer Ⓒ football Ⓓ golf

17. teacher : students :: _____ : team

Ⓐ trunk Ⓑ uniform Ⓒ coach Ⓓ box

18. invade : _____ :: protect : defend

Ⓐ attack Ⓑ hide Ⓒ retreat Ⓓ generals

19. puck : hockey stick :: baseball : _____

Ⓐ player Ⓑ cap Ⓒ bat Ⓓ stadium

20. baseball team : coach :: orchestra : _____

Ⓐ music Ⓑ score Ⓒ musicians Ⓓ conductor

21. playground : red rover :: swimming pool : _____

Ⓐ tag Ⓑ Marco Polo Ⓒ towel Ⓓ football

22. game : rules :: United States government : _____

Ⓐ judges Ⓑ Constitution Ⓒ penalties Ⓓ lawyers

23. question : inquiry :: agreement : _____

Ⓐ defense Ⓑ assent Ⓒ rebuke Ⓓ intent

24. command : order :: harness : _____

Ⓐ defend Ⓑ control Ⓒ hide Ⓓ discover

25. mission : goal :: diagram : _____

Ⓐ vehicle Ⓑ drawing Ⓒ partner Ⓓ jet pack

26. goal : soccer :: touchdown : _____

Ⓐ football Ⓑ basketball Ⓒ players Ⓓ swimming

27. United States : football :: England : _____
    - Ⓐ volleyball
    - Ⓑ polo
    - Ⓒ caddie
    - Ⓓ rugby

28. puck : hockey stick :: baseball : _____
    - Ⓐ stadium
    - Ⓑ bat
    - cap
    - Ⓓ player

29. winter : hockey :: spring : _____
    - Ⓐ baseball
    - Ⓑ diving
    - Ⓒ ice skating
    - Ⓓ football

30. phantom : ghost :: rival : _____
    - Ⓐ tourist
    - Ⓑ opponent
    - Ⓒ prank
    - Ⓓ friend

31. command : order :: harness : _____
    - Ⓐ hide
    - Ⓑ control
    - Ⓒ discover
    - Ⓓ defend

32. team : players :: choir : _____
    - Ⓐ singers
    - Ⓑ drums
    - Ⓒ instruments
    - Ⓓ band

33. game : rules :: United States government : _____
    - Ⓐ lawyers
    - Ⓑ penalties
    - Ⓒ judges
    - Ⓓ Constitution

34. game : rules :: United States government : _____
    - Ⓐ judges
    - Ⓑ penalties
    - Ⓒ lawyers
    - Ⓓ Constitution

35. falter : advance :: abandon : _____
    - Ⓐ hope
    - Ⓑ forward
    - Ⓒ rescue
    - Ⓓ lose

36. faddish : radish :: scrimmage : _____
    - Ⓐ football
    - Ⓑ scrimpy
    - Ⓒ image
    - Ⓓ caddish

37. football : quarterback :: basketball : _____
    - Ⓐ forward
    - Ⓑ center
    - Ⓒ guard
    - Ⓓ point guard

38. _____ : foul :: absurd : ludicrous
    - Ⓐ crazy
    - Ⓑ dirty
    - Ⓒ empty
    - Ⓓ mean

39. baseball team : coach :: orchestra : _____
    - Ⓐ musicians
    - Ⓑ music
    - Ⓒ conductor
    - Ⓓ score

40. dirty or disgusting : foul :: unpleasantly moist : _____
    - Ⓐ lathe
    - Ⓑ bogus
    - Ⓒ dank
    - Ⓓ mutant

41. basketball : dribble :: football : _____
    - (A) game
    - (B) jersey
    - (C) kick
    - (D) score

42. close : near :: far away : _____
    - (A) soon
    - (B) late
    - (C) score
    - (D) distant

43. win : conquered :: lose : _____
    - (A) tied
    - (B) scored
    - (C) defeated
    - (D) succeeded

44. to remove from a difficulty : extricate :: to secure with a rope : _____
    - (A) gyrate
    - (B) foul
    - (C) belay
    - (D) careen

45. seconds : time :: kilometers : _____
    - (A) weight
    - (B) wins
    - (C) score
    - (D) distance

46.. quick and light : nimble :: thick : _____
    - (A) dense
    - (B) crass
    - (C) foul
    - (D) drastic

47. falter : advance :: abandon : _____
    - (A) hope
    - (B) rescue
    - (C) forward
    - (D) lose

48. written material : _____ :: patented invention : infringement
    - (A) firewall
    - (B) hacking
    - (C) plagiarism
    - (D) peripherals

49. quick and light : nimble :: thick : _____
    - (A) dense
    - (B) crass
    - (C) drastic
    - (D) foul

50. close : near :: far away : _____
    - (A) soon
    - (B) distant
    - (C) score
    - (D) late

51. seconds : time :: kilometers : _____
    - (A) weight
    - (B) score
    - (C) wins
    - (D) distance

52. to remove from a difficulty : extricate :: to secure with a rope : _____
    - (A) belay
    - (B) gyrate
    - (C) careen
    - (D) foul

53. basketball : dribble :: football : _____
    - (A) game
    - (B) kick
    - (C) jersey
    - (D) score

54. football : quarterback :: basketball : _____
    - (A) point guard
    - (B) forward
    - (C) guard
    - (D) center

55. baseball team : coach :: orchestra : _____
    Ⓐ musicians   Ⓑ conductor   Ⓒ music   Ⓓ score

56. theatrical play : _____ :: orchestra : score
    Ⓐ voice lessons   Ⓑ memorizing   Ⓒ script   Ⓓ costumes

57. win : conquered :: lose : _____
    Ⓐ succeeded   Ⓑ tied   Ⓒ defeated   Ⓓ scored

58. dirty or disgusting : foul :: unpleasantly moist : _____
    Ⓐ lathe   Ⓑ bogus   Ⓒ mutant   Ⓓ dank

59. falter : advance :: abandon : _____
    Ⓐ forward   Ⓑ rescue   Ⓒ lose   ₌ hope

60. written material : _____ :: patented invention : infringement
    Ⓐ peripherals   Ⓑ firewall   Ⓒ hacking   Ⓓ plagiarism

61. seconds : time :: kilometers : _____
    Ⓐ wins   Ⓑ score   Ⓒ distance   Ⓓ weight

62. _____ : foul :: absurd : ludicrous
    Ⓐ mean   Ⓑ dirty   Ⓒ empty   Ⓓ crazy

63. quick and light : nimble :: thick : _____
    Ⓐ foul   Ⓑ dense   Ⓒ drastic   Ⓓ crass

64. win : conquered :: lose : _____
    Ⓐ tied   Ⓑ succeeded   Ⓒ defeated   Ⓓ scored

65. to remove from a difficulty : extricate :: to secure with a rope : _____
    Ⓐ careen   Ⓑ belay   Ⓒ foul   Ⓓ gyrate

66. written material : _____ :: patented invention : infringement
    Ⓐ peripherals   Ⓑ hacking   Ⓒ firewall   Ⓓ plagiarism

67. dirty or disgusting : foul :: unpleasantly moist : _____
    Ⓐ lathe   Ⓑ dank   Ⓒ bogus   Ⓓ mutant

68. close : near :: far away : _____
    Ⓐ soon   Ⓑ late   Ⓒ score   Ⓓ distant

69. falter : advance :: abandon : _____

 A) rescue   B) forward   C) hope   D) lose

70. theatrical play : _____ :: orchestra : score

 A) script   * memorizing   C) voice lessons   D) costumes

71. basketball : dribble :: football : _____

 A) jersey   B) score   C) game   D) kick

72. baseball team : coach :: orchestra : _____

 A) musicians   B) music   C) conductor   D) score

73. dismal : gloomy :: ample : _____

 A) plentiful   B) impressive   C) innovative   D) sturdy

74. stodgy : boring :: garish : _____

 A) flashy   B) courageous   C) gruesome   D) impressive

75. national : global :: _____ : celestial

 A) astronomical   B) ethereal   C) terrestrial   D) gravitational

76. podium : platform :: spigot : _____

 A) knob   B) rail   C) faucet   D) shelf

77. erroneous : mistaken :: imperative : _____

 A) required   B) impressive   C) honorable   D) professional

78. something that cannot be seen : invisible :: something that cannot be taken away : _____

 A) impressive   B) irrevocable   C) untoward   * indeterminable

79. conspire : plot :: consolidate : _____

 A) cover   B) trick   C) squeeze   D) combine

80. rostrum : podium :: oration : _____

 A) interment   B) speech   C) movie   D) confer

81. supplies : provisions :: pioneers : _____

 A) charters   B) settlers   C) initiatives   D) rations

82. deplorable : _____ :: imposing : impressive

     (A) confusing   **(B)** terrible   **(C)** fortunate   **(D)** great

83. joust : tournament :: peddler : _____

     (A) merchant   **(B)** poet   **(C)** farmer   **(D)** warrior

84. pioneers : settlers :: annoying animals : _____

     (A) citizens   **(B)** varmints   **(C)** pets   **(D)** traders

85. national : global :: _____ : celestial

     (A) astronomical   **(B)** ethereal   **(C)** terrestrial   **(D)** gravitational

86. dismal : gloomy :: ample : _____

     (A) plentiful   innovative   **(C)** sturdy   **(D)** impressive

87. deplorable : _____ :: imposing : impressive

     (A) confusing   **(B)** great   **(C)** fortunate   **(D)** terrible

88. something that cannot be seen : invisible :: something that cannot be taken away : _____

     (A) indeterminable   **(B)** untoward   **(C)** impressive   **(D)** irrevocable

89. melody : _____ :: headline : newspaper

     (A) book   **(B)** minister   **(C)** bells   **(D)** song

90. podium : platform :: spigot : _____

     (A) rail   **(B)** faucet   **(C)** shelf   **(D)** knob

91. prestigious : impressive :: ominous : _____

     (A) boring   **(B)** beautiful   **(C)** menacing   **(D)** doubtful

92. supplies : provisions :: pioneers : _____

     (A) settlers   **(B)** rations   **(C)** initiatives   **(D)** charters

93. conspire : plot :: consolidate : _____

     (A) cover   **(B)** combine   **(C)** trick   **(D)** squeeze

94. joust : tournament :: peddler : _____

     (A) merchant   **(B)** farmer   warrior   **(D)** poet

Team USA 2010

95. pioneers : settlers :: annoying animals : _____

    Ⓐ traders   Ⓑ varmints   Ⓒ pets   Ⓓ citizens

96. mouse : computer :: speaker : _____

    Ⓐ stereo   ⸱ podium   Ⓒ platform   Ⓓ kaleidoscope

97. conspire : plot :: consolidate : _____

    Ⓐ combine   ⸱ cover   Ⓒ trick   ⸱ squeeze

98. rostrum : podium :: oration : _____

    Ⓐ movie   Ⓑ interment   Ⓒ confer   Ⓓ speech

99. pioneers : settlers :: annoying animals : _____

    Ⓐ citizens   Ⓑ varmints   Ⓒ pets   Ⓓ traders

100. erroneous : mistaken :: imperative : _____

    Ⓐ impressive   Ⓑ required   Ⓒ professional   Ⓓ honorable

101. podium : platform :: spigot : _____

    Ⓐ rail   Ⓑ knob   Ⓒ shelf   Ⓓ faucet

102. dismal : gloomy :: ample : _____

    Ⓐ plentiful   Ⓑ sturdy   Ⓒ impressive   Ⓓ innovative

103. joust : tournament :: peddler : _____

    Ⓐ warrior   Ⓑ poet   Ⓒ merchant   Ⓓ farmer

104. prestigious : impressive :: ominous : _____

    ⸱ doubtful   Ⓑ boring   ⸱ beautiful   Ⓓ menacing

105. supplies : provisions :: pioneers : _____

    Ⓐ rations   Ⓑ settlers   Ⓒ charters   Ⓓ initiatives

106. something that cannot be seen : invisible :: something that cannot be taken away : _____

    Ⓐ impressive   Ⓑ irrevocable   Ⓒ untoward   Ⓓ indeterminable

107. melody : _____ :: headline : newspaper

    Ⓐ song   Ⓑ minister   Ⓒ book   Ⓓ bells

159

108. merciless : cruel :: vile : _____

Ⓐ repulsive   Ⓑ dangerous   Ⓒ impressive   Ⓓ kind

SECTION 5 WORD SEARCH & SENTENCES
Lesson 28

Answer Key 0202249

Complete each sentence using the words in the word list.

Francisco TORRES	Clarence GOODSON	Benny FEILHABER	Stuart Holden	Donovan
DaMarcus BEASLEY	Michael Bradley	Robbie FINDLEY	Oguchi ONYEWU	

_____1. ____ returned to the States from his unsuccessful English side, Sunderland, in 2006 and signed a contract with Houston Dynamo

_____2. In the 2007 SuperLiga tournament,____ was the top scorer. He scored a goal in every game except for the final.

_____3. It was not until after the 2008 Beijing Olympic Games in the Far East that ____ pledged his loyalty to the United States. Even then it looked as if he was leaning towards lining up for El Tri.

_____4. As of June 2010, ____, had scored 11 goals in 52 appearances with Norwegian club IK Start where he had established himself as a top defender in the Norwegian league.

_____5. ____ was a starter at the 2007 CONCACAF Gold Cup and helped lead the U.S. to the title, though he was sent off for a late tackle in the semifinal against Canada

_____6. At UCLA (in 2003) ____ was roommates with future national team-mate Jonathan Bornstein.

_____7. 6. Shortly after making his debut with the southern California side, ____ was sent off to Real Salt Lake, where he helped make the Utah-based outsiders league champions in 2009.

_____8. As of July 2010, ____ had scored more goals in Europe's highest club competition, the UEFA Champions League, than any other American player

_____9. According to South Africa 2010 FIFA sports report ____ "looks more like an American gridiron player than a footballer but he gives Bob Bradley's USA size, power and a bite at the back"

161

Answer Key 0202249

Complete each sentence using the words in the word list.

Jonathan BORNSTEIN	Francisco TORRES	Robbie FINDLEY	Jozy ALTIDORE
Jonathan SPECTOR	Clarence GOODSON	Landon DONOVAN	Guzan

_____ 10. The skilful attacking midfielder, ____, has since 1999 earned over 100 caps and become USA's top all-time scorer.

_____ 11. 7. He was discovered by Manchester United scout Jimmy Ryan while playing for the American Under-17 squad at the Milk Cup in 2003. With Manchester United, ____ made a number of appearances from the start and off the bench.

_____ 12. He began his professional playing career with FC Dallas in 2004 after three years of successfully playing at college level. In four seasons with his Texas club, FC Dallas ____ made 76 appearances and his leaping ability saw him grab the odd goal as well on set-pieces.

_____ 13. He was recruited early on as a teenager to play for Mexican outfit Pachuca. José ____ was recruited by Pachuca while he was still attending high school in Texas.

_____ 14. 6. In the South Africa 2010 FIFA World Cup ____ started at left back against Algeria in the final group play game and against Ghana in the round of sixteen after sitting out the first two group-stage games for the United States.

_____ 15. 5. After a successful University career, the jet-heeled striker, ____, moved on to USA's lower leagues before settling into MLS with LA Galaxy in 2007.

_____ 16. With roots in the Caribbean nation of Haiti, ____, just 19, began his professional career with a bang in the domestic top flight with 15 goals in 37 appearances over two seasons for New York Red Bulls.

_____ 17. Since 2006,____ has established himself as the second-choice goalkeeper for the United States national team behind Everton's Tim Howard.

Answer Key 0202249

Complete each sentence using the words in the word list.

DaMarcus Beasley	Jonathan SPECTOR	Benny FEILHABER	Stuart Holden	Maurice Edu
Steve CHERUNDOLO	Michael BRADLEY	Landon DONOVAN	Oguchi Onyewu	

_____18. ____ was named to the Belgian league's Best XI as well as Foreign Player of the Year for 2005. On December 26, 2006, he was voted U.S. Soccer Athlete of the Year. He was the first defender to earn the award since Alexi Lalas in 1995.

_____19. ____ played for the Under-20 team at the 2001 World Youth Championship in Argentina.

_____20. ____ made his Major League Soccer debut on 25 April 2007, against Kansas City Wizards.

_____21. He arrived at organized collegiate football in the USA in a most unusual way. ____ first enrolled at the University of California, Los Angeles, but he was not recruited to play soccer.

_____22. 4. After an outstanding career with the United States youth national team set-up, lining up at FIFA U-17 World Cup in Finland in 2003, ____ was already chipping away at a club career abroad.

_____23. Although then not yet a member of the US squad, ____ was brought into the World Cup 2006 training camp in Cary, North Carolina to train with the United States national team.

_____24. In 2005, English Premier League side Bolton Wanderers F.C. agreed to a deal with Hannover for _____, but he declined, opting to remain in Germany. He signed contract extensions with Hannover in the summers of 2007 and 2010.

_____25. In his first season with the Galaxy, ____ scored twelve league goals and ten assists.

_____26. ____ is the Scottish-born player who is able to play in an attacking-midfield role or out wide on the right.

163

Answer Key 0202249

Complete each sentence using the words in the word list.

Michael Bradley	Jozy Altidore	Ricardo CLARK	Edson BUDDLE	Jay DeMERIT
Robbie Findley	Clint Dempsey	Bradley Guzan	Jay DeMerit	

_____27. When Howard was suspended for a match at El Salvador due to accumulated yellow cards, ____ started and helped U.S. earn a critical 2-2 draw.

_____28. Born in the frost-covered American north in Wisconsin, ____, the then powerful Chicago Fire Premier defender headed over to Europe on a wing and a prayer and soon made a name for himself in England.

_____29. ____ played on the 2010 World Cup US Team as one of four forwards and was tipped by many to fill the gap for USA left by the retirement of former icon Brian McBride.

_____30. From the Columbus Crew, ____ moved to New York Red Bulls and later to Toronto FC but the fleet-footed striker failed to recreate the good form he had in Columbus.

_____31. ____ started every match for the U.S. at the 2007 FIFA U-20 World Cup, where he scored the game-winning goal in the 107th minute against Uruguay in the round of 16.

_____32. ____ joined a semi-pro side in England before impressing and signing with Watford, where he played a season in the English Premier League (2007-2008).

_____33. 1.____'s form for Real Salt Lake put him on the national team coach's radar in the run-up to South Africa.

_____34. As a soccer player ____ was a tireless worker in the middle of the park. His exuberance, energy and youthful graft made him a useful option for US coach, Bob Bradley.

_____35. ____ attended Furman University as a health and exercise major and a key player for the Paladins.

Answer Key 0202249

Complete each sentence using the words in the word list.

Jonathan BORNSTEIN	Steve CHERUNDOLO	Robbie FINDLEY	Brad GUZAN
DaMarcus Beasley	Herculez Gomez	Oguchi Onyewu	

_____36. 3. At Oregon State University ____ earned All-Pacific-10 honors in all four seasons and was the Pac-10 (college athletic conference) Freshman of the Year in 2003.

_____37. At 25, ____ had risen fast in the competitive world of big league goalkeeping, where patience and experience often trumps ability.

_____38. Although ____ was on Team USA roster for the 2002 FIFA World Cup after a late injury replacement for Chris Armas, he himself was injured in training shortly before the event began and was unable to play.

_____39. As an American Youth soccer star, ____ has bee an American success story overseas for a full decade now. He was a sturdy and reliable right-back for Team USA.

_____40. 5. In 2008, ____ lost his starting place to Heath Pearce and also struggled with injuries. He started the group stage matches at the 2009 FIFA Confederations Cup but was relegated back to the bench when Carlos Bocanegra returned from injury.

_____41. ____ was loaned to Manchester City in 2006, and later signed by Rangers in June 2007 for £700,000.

_____42. ____ signed with Mexican club Puebla F.C. in January 2010 and scored ten goals in the 2010 Mexican season to tie for the lead for most goals; a feat which marked the first time any American player led a foreign league in goals.

_____43. ____ made his debut for Newcastle against Fulham on February 3, 2007, and his home debut a week later, alongside Titus Bramble, in a 2–1 victory over Liverpool.

Answer Key 0202249

Complete each sentence using the words in the word list.

Jonathan BORNSTEIN	Francisco TORRES	Herculez Gomez	Stuart HOLDEN	Edson BUDDLE
Herculez Gomez's	Michael Bradley	Bradley Guzan	Jozy ALTIDORE	DeMerit

_____44. ____ was an outsider to make Bob Bradley's final squad for the 2010 FIFA World Cup South Africa™.

_____45. At 29, ____ had yet to figure prominently in the US national team set-up, but his nose for goal and fine form for LA Galaxy in the run-up to South Africa 2010 made him a dangerous joker for his coach.

_____46. As a high schooler, ____ attended Boca Prep before joining the U.S. U-17 Residency program.

_____47. By June 2010, at 24, ____ had established himself as a versatile option for Bob Bradley's US side ahead of the 2010 FIFA World Cup™.

_____48. ____ started the USA's 3-0 win over Egypt in the 2009 Confederations Cup.

_____49. With nearly 170 appearances at Watford, ____ earned the right to wear Watford F.C 's armband on occasion .

_____50. At the 2008 Summer Olympics in Beijing, ____ was invited by Peter Nowak, a Polish former professional soccer player and the head coach of the Philadelphia Union in Major League Soccer, to play for the United States U-23 team

_____51. 3. On January 20, 2007 ____ got his first cap, and first goal on an assist from Justin Mapp, for the U.S. national team against Denmark.

_____52. ____ earned his first international cap in the May 26, 2006 match against Venezuela as a substitute and his second cap for the United States in the following game against Latvia, again as a substitute.

_____53. ____ hot form at club level in Mexico was something Coach Bob Bradley simply could not ignore.

Answer Key 0202249

Complete each sentence using the words in the word list.

Clarence GOODSON	Ricardo Clark	Maurice Edu	DeMerit
Benny FEILHABER	Clint DEMPSEY	Donovan	Edu's

_____54. Having played and impressed at MLS level, the tall defender, ____, is making a go of football in Scandinavia with Norwegian side IK Start.

_____55. In December 2006, Fulham offered MLS a $4 million transfer fee for ____, then the largest amount ever offered for an MLS player.

_____56. In 1996, as a youth soccer player ____ led the team and won the New York State Cup for the U-12 division.

_____57. Back from a two-goal, second-half deficit to stage US's greatest World Cup comeback and earn a remarkable 2-2 draw with Slovenia,____ goal which would have tallied the winner was nullified by referee Koman Coulibaly of Mali without giving an explanation as to what exactly happened.

_____58. ____ had a confident opening season and turned more than a few heads in the Big Apple during his professional career with the MetroStars (now the New York Red Bulls) in 2003.

_____59. In July 2004,____ joined Northwood, a seventh-tier side, to play in some of their pre-season matches. Northwood played Championship side Watford, then a League Championship side in their second pre-season match. During the course of the match, he impressed then Watford manager Ray Lewin

_____60. ____ was at the University of Maryland, College Park from 2004 until 2006 and played three years for the Maryland Terrapins, including a role on the 2005 squad which won the NCAA College Cup national championship.

_____61. Playing along with David Beckham at Los Angeles Galaxy in 2009,____ enjoyed an outstanding 2009 campaign, winning the league's Most Valuable Player and MLS Goal of The Year 2009 award.

Answer Key 0202249
Complete each sentence using the words in the word list.

| Francisco Torres | Jonathan SPECTOR | Ricardo Clark |
| Steve CHERUNDOLO | Edson Buddle's | Edson Buddle |

_____ 62. 5. He joined up with world football giants Manchester United in 2001 as a teenager. At Manchester United ____ made a handful of appearances for Sir Alex Ferguson's first team, before being sent out on loan to Charlton Athletic in 2005.

_____ 63. ____ was a surprise inclusion in USA's squad for the 2010 FIFA World Cup South Africa™ to fill the hole left by injured striker Charlie Davies.

_____ 64. ____, the Atlanta, Georgia native began his professional career with the MetroStars (now the New York Red Bulls) in 2003, where he was one of the finalists for the 'rookie of the year' award in Major League Soccer.

_____ 65. ____ addition to the US national team would compensate for the loss of the LA Galaxy striker Charlie Davies for South Africa 2010. It was hoped that his explosive pace will enhance US's prospects in the absence of injured striker Charlie Davies.

_____ 66. ____ eventually broke into the starting line-up for his for Mexican outfit' Pachuca, in 2008, where he played all three games for the club at the FIFA Club World Cup in Japan.

_____ 67. Strong, dependable and with a sharp positional sense ____ had the desire to get up into attack.

_____ 68. ____ has played for several youth United States national teams including the 2003 World Youth Championship in the United Arab Emirates.

_____ 69. 3. At 24, ____'s emergence in English football was nothing short of meteoric. However injuries have since his 24th birthday blighted his rise and limited his playing time, he is still a useful option open to USA head coach Bob Bradley in defence.

Answer Key 0202249

Complete each sentence using the words in the word list.

Jonathan Bornstein	Clarence Goodson	Herculez GOMEZ	Stuart HOLDEN
DaMarcus Beasley's	Jozy Altidore's	Clint Dempsey	Clint DEMPSEY

_____ 70. With only a handful of US caps to his name, the then 28-year-old striker, ____, who is of joint Mexican-American ancestry had a breakout season with Mexican outfit Puebla in 2010.

_____ 71. ____ emergence on the American soccer scene began way back in 2000, when he lined up for Chicago Fire of Major League Soccer after shining for the USA's U-17 national team at the junior FIFA World Cup in New Zealand in the summer.

_____ 72. ____ first played for the American national team at the 2003 FIFA World Youth Championship in the United Arab Emirates and made his first appearance with the senior team on November 17, 2004 against Jamaica.

_____ 73. He played two years of college soccer at Clemson University before signing with English club Sunderland in March 2005. An ill-fated move to English side Sunderland in 2005 ended without making even one appearance for the club.

_____ 74. 7.____ scored the equalizing goal in the United States' final World Cup qualifier against Costa Rica in the fifth minute of injury time.

_____ 75. ____ was well needed by USA coach Bob Bradley with normal starter Oguchi Onyewu still recovering from a knee injury on the eve of the 2010 FIFA World Cup South Africa™.

_____ 76. ____ is a versatile attacking player for the US national soccer team known for his ball skills with an eye for goal and keen dribbling ability.

_____ 77. ____ power, nose for goal and ability to bring those around him into the game and disrupt opposition defences was soon attracting the attention of one of Europe's top talent assessors, former Real Madrid coach Manuel Pellegrini.

SECTION 6: CHOOSE THE RIGHT ANSWERS
Lesson 29
Answer Key 0283320

Complete each sentence.

_____1. **(Benny FEILHABER, Michael BRADLEY,_Oguchi ONYEWU)** was named to the Belgian league's Best XI as well as Foreign Player of the Year for 2005. On December 26, 2006, he was voted U.S. Soccer Athlete of the Year. He was the first defender to earn the award since Alexi Lalas in 1995.

_____2. In 1996, as a youth soccer player **(Benny Feilhaber, Stuart HOLDEN, Edson BUDDLE)** led the team and won the New York State Cup for the U-12 division.

_____3. He made the college soccer team as a walk-on, rather than being recruited with a scholarship offer. However after his second year at **UCLA (Benny FEILHABER, Brad GUZAN, Herculez GOMEZ)** was called up by the U.S. U-20 national soccer team to play in the 2005 FIFA World Youth Championship in the Netherlands.

_____4. 7. He was discovered by Manchester United scout Jimmy Ryan while playing for the American Under-17 squad at the Milk Cup in 2003. With Manchester United, **(Clarence GOODSON, Oguchi ONYEWU, Jonathan Spector)** made a number of appearances from the start and off the bench.

_____5. **(Jonathan BORNSTEIN, Herculez Gomez , Brad GUZAN)** signed with Mexican club Puebla F.C. in January 2010 and scored ten goals in the 2010 Mexican season to tie for the lead for most goals; a feat which marked the first time any American player led a foreign league in goals.

_____6. In July 2004, **(DaMarcus BEASLEY, Robbie FINDLEY, DeMerit)** joined Northwood, a seventh-tier side, to play in some of their pre-season matches. Northwood played Championship side Watford, then a League Championship side in their second pre-season match. During the course of the match, DeMerit impressed then Watford manager Ray Lewin.

_____7. **(Jozy Altidore's, Edson BUDDLE, Herculez GOMEZ)** power, nose for goal and ability to bring those around him into the game and disrupt opposition defences was soon attracting the attention of one of Europe's top talent assessors, former Real Madrid coach Manuel Pellegrini.

Answer Key 0283320

Complete each sentence.

_____ 8. 6. In the South Africa 2010 FIFA World Cup **(Jonathan Bornstein, Steve CHERUNDOLO, Jay DeMERIT)** started at left back against Algeria in the final group play game and against Ghana in the round of sixteen after sitting out the first two group-stage games for the United States.

_____ 9. **(Francisco Torres, Brad GUZAN, Jay DeMERIT)** eventually broke into the starting line-up for his for Mexican outfit' Pachuca, in 2008, where he played all three games for the club at the FIFA Club World Cup in Japan.

_____ 10. 1. **(Clint DEMPSEY, Robbie Findley , Ricardo CLARK)** 's form for Real Salt Lake put him on the national team coach's radar in the run-up to South Africa.

_____ 11. He arrived at organized collegiate football in the USA in a most unusual way. **(Jay DeMERIT, Benny Feilhaber, Jonathan BORNSTEIN)** first enrolled at the University of California, Los Angeles, but he was not recruited to play soccer.

_____ 12. At the 2008 Summer Olympics in Beijing, **(Francisco Torres, Clarence GOODSON, Jonathan BORNSTEIN)** was invited by Peter Nowak, a Polish former professional soccer player and the head coach of the Philadelphia Union in Major League Soccer, to play for the United States U-23 team

_____ 13. The skilful attacking midfielder, **(Landon Donovan, Edson BUDDLE, Steve CHERUNDOLO)**, has since 1999 earned over 100 caps and become USA's top all-time scorer.

_____ 14. In 2005, English Premier League side Bolton Wanderers F.C. agreed to a deal with Hannover for him, but he declined, opting to remain in Germany. **(Ricardo CLARK, Maurice EDU, Steve Cherundolo)** signed contract extensions with Hannover in the summers of 2007 and 2010.

Answer Key 0283320
Complete each sentence.

_____15. **(Landon DONOVAN, Jay DeMerit , Maurice EDU)** joined a semi-pro side in England before impressing and signing with Watford, where he played a season in the English Premier League (2007-2008).

_____16. In the 2007 SuperLiga tournament, **(Donovan, Jonathan BORNSTEIN, Robbie FINDLEY)** was the top scorer. He scored a goal in every game except for the final.

_____17. **(Clint Dempsey, Robbie FINDLEY, Francisco TORRES)** first played for the American national team at the 2003 FIFA World Youth Championship in the United Arab Emirates and made his first appearance with the senior team on November 17, 2004 against Jamaica.

_____18. **(Clint DEMPSEY, Stuart HOLDEN, DaMarcus Beasley)** was loaned to Manchester City in 2006, and later signed by Rangers in June 2007 for £700,000.

_____19. Back from a two-goal, second-half deficit to stage US's greatest World Cup comeback and earn a remarkable 2-2 draw with Slovenia, **(Jay DeMERIT's, Stuart HOLDEN's, Maurice Edu's)** goal which would have tallied the winner was nullified by referee Koman Coulibaly of Mali without giving an explanation as to what exactly happened.

_____20. Having played and impressed at MLS level, the tall defender, **(Ricardo CLARK, Clarence Goodson, Stuart HOLDEN)**, is making a go of football in Scandinavia with Norwegian side IK Start.

_____21. According to South Africa 2010 FIFA sports report **(Oguchi Onyewu, Edson BUDDLE, Stuart HOLDEN)** "looks more like an American gridiron player than a footballer but he gives Bob Bradley's USA size, power and a bite at the back"

_____22. Strong, dependable and with a sharp positional sense **(Clint DEMPSEY, Francisco TORRES, Steve Cherundolo)** had the desire to get up into attack.

Answer Key 0283320

Complete each sentence.

_____ 23. With roots in the Caribbean nation of Haiti, **(Jay DeMERIT, Francisco TORRES, Jozy Altidore)**, just 19, began his professional career with a bang in the domestic top flight with 15 goals in 37 appearances over two seasons for New York Red Bulls.

_____ 24. **(Ricardo CLARK, Landon DONOVAN, Michael Bradley)** was a starter at the 2007 CONCACAF Gold Cup and helped lead the U.S. to the title, though he was sent off for a late tackle in the semifinal against Canada

_____ 25. 5. He joined up with world football giants Manchester United in 2001 as a teenager. At Manchester United **(DaMarcus BEASLEY, Jonathan Spector, Landon DONOVAN)** made a handful of appearances for Sir Alex Ferguson's first team, before being sent out on loan to Charlton Athletic in 2005.

_____ 26. At UCLA (in 2003) **(Clarence GOODSON, Francisco TORRES, Benny Feilhaber)** was roommates with future national team-mate Jonathan Bornstein.

_____ 27. **(Jozy ALTIDORE, Michael Bradley, Stuart HOLDEN)** started every match for the U.S. at the 2007 FIFA U-20 World Cup, where he scored the game-winning goal in the 107th minute against Uruguay in the round of 16.

_____ 28. **(Herculez GOMEZ, Jonathan BORNSTEIN, Ricardo CLARK)** has played for several youth United States national teams including the 2003 World Youth Championship in the United Arab Emirates.

_____ 29. With nearly 170 appearances at Watford, **(Clint DEMPSEY, Oguchi ONYEWU, DeMerit)** earned the right to wear Watford F.C 's armband on occasion.

_____ 30. **(Jozy ALTIDORE, DaMarcus BEASLEY, Clarence Goodson)** was well needed by USA coach Bob Bradley with normal starter Oguchi Onyewu still recovering from a knee injury on the eve of the 2010 FIFA World Cup South Africa™.

Answer Key 0283320

Complete each sentence.

_____31. 3. At 24, **(Jonathan Spector, Maurice EDU, Brad GUZAN)** 's emergence in English football was nothing short of meteoric. However injuries have since his 24th birthday blighted his rise and limited his playing time. He is still a useful option open to USA head coach Bob Bradley in defence.

_____32. **(Bradley Guzan, Benny FEILHABER, Herculez GOMEZ)** started the USA's 3-0 win over Egypt in the 2009 Confederations Cup.

_____33. As a soccer player **(Ricardo Clark, Maurice EDU, Robbie FINDLEY)** was a tireless worker in the middle of the park. His exuberance, energy and youthful graft made him a useful option for US coach, Bob Bradley.

_____34. **(DaMarcus Beasley's, Oguchi ONYEWU's, Jonathan's SPECTOR)** emergence on the American soccer scene began way back in 2000, when he lined up for Chicago Fire of Major League Soccer after shining for the USA's U-17 national team at the junior FIFA World Cup in New Zealand in the summer.

_____35. As of June 2010, **(Jonathan SPECTOR, Clarence Goodson, Benny FEILHABER)**, had scored 11 goals in 52 appearances with Norwegian club IK Start where he had established himself as a top defender in the Norwegian league.

_____36. In his first season with the Galaxy, **(Oguchi ONYEWU, Landon Donovan, Maurice EDU)** scored twelve league goals and ten assists.

_____37. 5. After a successful University career, the jet-heeled striker, **(Landon DONOVAN, Steve CHERUNDOLO, Robbie Findley)**, moved on to USA's lower leagues before settling into MLS with LA Galaxy in 2007.

_____38. **(Herculez Gomez, Robbie FINDLEY, Jay DeMERIT)** was an outsider to make Bob Bradley's final squad for the 2010 FIFA World Cup South Africa™.

_____39. **(Clint Dempsey, Edson BUDDLE, Oguchi ONYEWU)** attended Furman University as a health and exercise major and a key player for the Paladins.

Answer Key 0283320

Complete each sentence.

_____ 40. **(Clint DEMPSEY, Jonathan SPECTOR, Maurice Edu)** was at the University of Maryland, College Park from 2004 until 2006 and played three years for the Maryland Terrapins, including a role on the 2005 squad which won the NCAA College Cup national championship.

_____ 41. Since 2006, **(Clint DEMPSEY, Edson BUDDLE, Guzan)** has established himself as the second-choice goalkeeper for the United States national team behind Everton's Tim Howard.

_____ 42. Although **(Jonathan SPECTOR, DaMarcus BEASLEY, Steve Cherundolo)** was on Team USA roster for the 2002 FIFA World Cup after a late injury replacement for Chris Armas, Cherundolo himself was injured in training shortly before the event began and was unable to play.

_____ 43. In 2008, **(Herculez GOMEZ, Maurice EDU, Jonathan Bornstein)** lost his starting place to Heath Pearce and also struggled with injuries. He started the group stage matches at the 2009 FIFA Confederations Cup but was relegated back to the bench when Carlos Bocanegra returned from injury.

_____ 44. **(Stuart HOLDEN, Benny FEILHABER, Jozy Altidore)** played on the 2010 World Cup US Team as one of four forwards and was tipped by many to fill the gap for USA left by the retirement of former icon Brian McBride.

_____ 45. After an outstanding career with the United States youth national team set-up, lining up at FIFA U-17 World Cup in Finland in 2003, **(Michael BRADLEY, Clint DEMPSEY, Jonathan Spector)** was already chipping away at a club career abroad.

_____ 46. **(Francisco TORRES, Brad GUZAN, Oguchi Onyewu)** made his debut for Newcastle against Fulham on February 3, 2007, and his home debut a week later, alongside Titus Bramble, in a 2–1 victory over Liverpool.

_____ 47. By June 2010, at 24, **(DaMarcus BEASLEY, Stuart Holden, Steve CHERUNDOLO)** had established himself as a versatile option for Bob Bradley's US side ahead of the 2010 FIFA World Cup™.

Answer Key 0283320

Complete each sentence.

_____48. **(Brad GUZAN, Landon DONOVAN, Maurice Edu)** made his Major League Soccer debut on 25 April 2007, against Kansas City Wizards.

_____49. As an American Youth soccer star, **(Steve Cherundolo, Clarence GOODSON, Oguchi ONYEWU)** has bee an American success story overseas for a full decade now. He was a sturdy and reliable right-back for Team USA.

_____50. In 2003, **(DaMarcus BEASLEY, Jozy ALTIDORE, Oguchi Onyewu)** was loaned out to La Louvière in Belgium, and to Standard Liège a year later; the move to Liège was made permanent for the 2004–05 season.

_____51. It was not until after the 2008 Beijing Olympic Games in the Far East that **(Francisco Torres, Robbie FINDLEY, Landon DONOVAN)** pledged his loyalty to the United States. Even then it looked as if he was leaning towards lining up for El Tri.

_____52. 3. At Oregon State University **(Brad GUZAN, Jonathan BORNSTEIN, Robbie Findley)** earned All-Pacific-10 honors in all four seasons and was the Pac-10 (college athletic conference) Freshman of the Year in 2003.

_____53. **(Maurice Edu, Michael BRADLEY, DaMarcus BEASLEY)** scored his first professional goal in the seventy-fifth minute of a game against Chicago Fire on May 12, 2007.

_____54. Playing along with David Beckham at Los Angeles Galaxy in 2009, **(Herculez GOMEZ, Donovan, Francisco TORRES)** enjoyed an outstanding 2009 campaign, winning the league's Most Valuable Player and MLS Goal of The Year 2009 award.

_____55. In December 2006, Fulham offered MLS a $4 million transfer fee for **(Jozy ALTIDORE, Clint Dempsey, Benny FEILHABER)**, then the largest amount ever offered for an MLS player.

Answer Key 0283320

Complete each sentence.

56. **(Robbie FINDLEY, Stuart Holden , Oguchi ONYEWU)** returned to the States from his unsuccessful English side, Sunderland, in 2006 and signed a contract with Houston Dynamo

57. **(Jonathan BORNSTEIN, Clint DEMPSEY, Michael Bradley)** earned his first international cap in the May 26, 2006 match against Venezuela as a substitute and his second cap for the United States in the following game against Latvia, again as a substitute.

58. As a high schooler, **(Jonathan BORNSTEIN, Ricardo CLARK, Jozy Altidore)** attended Boca Prep before joining the U.S. U-17 Residency program.

59. From the Columbus Crew, **(Edson Buddle, Michael BRADLEY, Jozy ALTIDORE)** moved to New York Red Bulls and later to Toronto FC but the fleet-footed striker failed to recreate the good form he had in Columbus.

60. **(Ricardo Clark, Clarence GOODSON, Clint DEMPSEY)**, the Atlanta, Georgia native began his professional career with the MetroStars (now the New York Red Bulls) in 2003, where he was one of the finalists for the 'rookie of the year' award in Major League Soccer.

61. **(DaMarcus BEASLEY, Stuart HOLDEN, Edson Buddle)** was a surprise inclusion in USA's squad for the 2010 FIFA World Cup South Africa™ to fill the hole left by injured striker Charlie Davies.

62. **(Oguchi ONYEWU, Steve CHERUNDOLO, Ricardo Clark)** had a confident opening season and turned more than a few heads in the Big Apple during his professional career with the MetroStars (now the New York Red Bulls) in 2003.

63. **(Jonathan BORNSTEIN, Clint Dempsey, Clarence GOODSON)** is a versatile attacking player for the US national soccer team known for his ball skills with an eye for goal and keen dribbling ability.

177

Answer Key 0283320

Complete each sentence.

_____ 64. **(Herculez GOMEZ's, Oguchi ONYEWU's, Edson Buddle's)** addition to the US national team would compensate for the loss of t the LA Galaxy striker Charlie Davies for South Africa 2010. It was hoped that his explosive pace will enhance US's prospects in the absence of injured striker Charlie Davies.

_____ 65. 3. On January 20, 2007 **(Jonathan SPECTOR, Benny FEILHABER, Jonathan Bornstein)** got his first cap, and first goal on an assist from Justin Mapp, for the U.S. national team against Denmark.

_____ 66. **(Jozy ALTIDORE's, Herculez Gomez's, Benny FEILHABER's)** hot form at club level in Mexico was something Coach Bob Bradley simply could not ignore.

_____ 67. **(Brad GUZAN, Jonathan Bornstein, Robbie FINDLEY)** scored the equalizing goal in the United States' final World Cup qualifier against Costa Rica in the fifth minute of injury time.

_____ 68. **(Herculez GOMEZ, Jozy ALTIDORE, DaMarcus Beasley)** played for the Under-20 team at the 2001 World Youth Championship in Argentina.

_____ 69. Born in the frost-covered American north in Wisconsin, **(Jay DeMerit, Steve CHERUNDOLO, Ricardo CLARK)**, the then powerful Chicago Fire Premier defender headed over to Europe on a wing and a prayer and soon made a name for himself in England.

_____ 70. At 29, **(Francisco TORRES, Edson Buddle, Clarence GOODSON)** had yet to figure prominently in the US national team set-up, but his nose for goal and fine form for LA Galaxy in the run-up to South Africa 2010 made him a dangerous joker for his coach.

_____ 71. When Howard was suspended for a match at El Salvador due to accumulated yellow cards, **(Jonathan SPECTOR, Bradley Guzan, Maurice EDU)** started and helped U.S. earn a critical 2-2 draw.

178

SECTION 7: SCRAMBLE WORDS

Lesson 30
Answer Key 0307885

Unscramble the words.

1. BADR NUGZA _____	2. JAY IRDMEET _____
3. SDONE ULDEBD _____	4. ONCRFCAIS TEORRS _____
5. CEELCARN DSNGOOO _____	6. TCNLI SEEDYMP _____
7. OJZY TRDLEOAI _____	8. RUACEMI UDE _____
9. DCORRIA LARKC _____	10. ECMIALH REYBADL _____
11. GHIUOC YENOUW _____	12. TEESV NRDOUELCOH _____
13. ASURTT EDOLHN _____	14. NENBY EHFBIAREL _____
15. EBOIBR LNEFDIY _____	16. ANDOLN NOANVOD _____
17. NHOJATNA BTNESIRNO _____	18. JNANOAHT ORCESTP _____
19. LEZRECHU ZGMOE _____	20. MSUCAARD SBEAELY _____

VOCABULARY

21. EFDOLD _____	22. LIENEHDA _____
23. AEDRTEEGL _____	24. MOAUENRTTN _____
25. OACISDETNLOD _____	26. POIDUM _____

179

27.	28.
GBOALL _____	**ENIPORSE** _____

SECTION 8: WORD PUZZLES

Lesson 31	
Answer Key 20694974	

Word List

Benny FEILHABER	Edson BUDDLE	Jonathan SPECTOR	Oguchi ONYEWU
Brad GUZAN	Francisco TORRES	Jozy ALTIDORE	Ricardo CLARK
Clarence GOODSON	Herculez GOMEZ	Landon DONOVAN	Robbie FINDLEY
Clint DEMPSEY	Jay DeMERIT	Maurice EDU	Steve CHERUNDOLO
DaMarcus BEASLEY	Jonathan BORNSTEIN	Michael BRADLEY	Stuart HOLDEN

Complete each sentence using the correct word

Down

1. In his first season with the Galaxy, ___ scored twelve league goals and ten assists.
   (2 words)
3. At 25, ___ had risen fast in the competitive world of big league goalkeeping, where patience and experience often trumps ability.
   (2 words)

Across

2. From the Columbus Crew, ___ moved to New York Red Bulls and later to Toronto FC but the fleet-footed striker failed to recreate the good form he had in Columbus.
   (2 words)
4. As a soccer player ___ was a tireless worker in the middle of the park. His exuberance, energy and youthful graft made him a useful option for US coach, Bob Bradley.

   (2 words)

20694974

Find only those words that complete the sentences in the word search

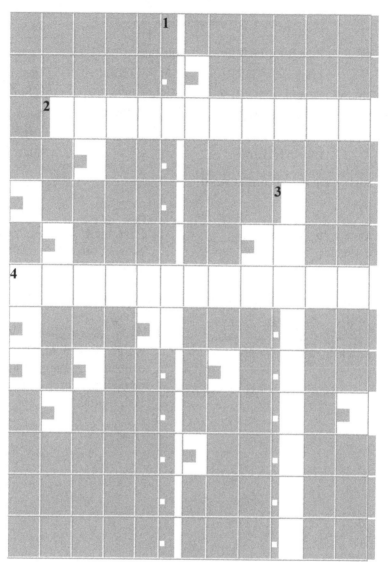

Cross Word Puzzle
Answer Key 21705985

Name _____   Date _____

Choose the word that is the most nearly the same in meaning as the list of synonyms. A word should not be used more than once.

Word List		
Consolidated	Global	Podium
Folded	Headline	Tournament

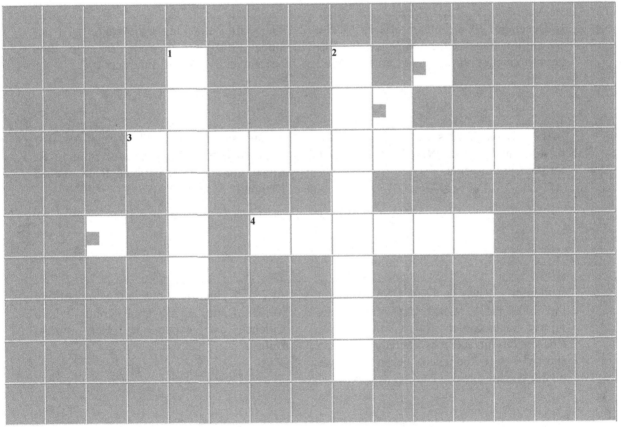

Down
1. fixed, omnibus, definite, comprehensive, cosmopolitan, ecumenical, universal, unequivocal
2. drop head, bomb, open, star

Across
3. competition, tourney, contest, meet, challenge, go, games, match, series, match, competition
4. pliable, flexible

Answer Key 0694974
Word List

Benny FEILHABER	Edson BUDDLE	Jonathan SPECTOR	Oguchi ONYEWU
Brad GUZAN	Francisco TORRES	Jozy ALTIDORE	Ricardo CLARK
Clarence GOODSON	Herculez GOMEZ	Landon DONOVAN	Robbie FINDLEY
Clint DEMPSEY	Jay DeMERIT	Maurice EDU	Steve
DaMarcus BEASLEY	Jonathan BORNSTEIN	Michael BRADLEY	CHERUNDOLO Stuart HOLDEN

Using this word list, figure out which words complete the sentences.

Answer Key 0694974

Complete each sentence using the correct word.
Then find the correct form in the word search.

1. In December 2006, Fulham offered MLS a $4 million transfer fee for ___ , then the largest amount ever offered for an MLS player.	2. The skilful attacking midfielder, ___ , has since 1999 earned over 100 caps and become USA's top all-time scorer.
3. In 1996, as a youth soccer player ___ led the team and won the New York State Cup for the U-12 division.	4. 3. On January 20, 2007 ___ got his first cap, and first goal on an assist from Justin Mapp, for the U.S. national team against Denmark.
5. Although ___ was on Team USA roster for the 2002 FIFA World Cup after a late injury replacement for Chris Armas, Cherundolo himself was injured in training shortly before the event began and was unable to play.	6. At 25, ___ had risen fast in the competitive world of big league goalkeeping, where patience and experience ·often trumps ability.
7. As a soccer player ___ was a tireless worker in the middle of the park. His exuberance, energy and youthful graft made him a useful option for US coach, Bob Bradley.	8. At 29, ___ had yet to figure prominently in the US national team set-up, but his nose for goal and fine form for LA Galaxy in the run-up to South Africa 2010 made him a dangerous joker for his coach.

184

9. 4. After an outstanding career with the United States youth national team set-up, lining up at FIFA U-17 World Cup in Finland in 2003, ___ was already chipping away at a club career abroad.	10. As of July 2010, ___ had scored more goals in Europe's highest club competition, the UEFA Champions League, than any other American player

Find only those words that completed the sentences in the word search

Answer Key 0694974

```
E A L M N E I T S N R O B   N A H T A N O J  O H
L N   B E I H T J U N I  H N B R A   G U Z A N E
D T M   A T L R   A E N C N E Z R E A S A A A A
D   R D R E I B Z T O K R A L   O D R A C I  R A
U C A S B B A U O I A N A Y R   S A Y H Y O H N
B R H E O S G O L A N D O N   D O N O V A N Y U
  R T Y L   D D N A V O N O D   O D N A L E R T
N   T R D N N O E R E B A H L I  F   Y N N E B E
O J C A C L I N T   D E M P S E Y C T D E C E
S N R Y E S P M E D   T N I  L C L S N L C M T A
D B J O N A T H A N   B O R N S T E I N A N Y T
E I B E N N Y   F E I L H A B E R C A B N R A L
D A M A R C U S   B E A S L E Y M O I E O A K F
D N U I  V S T E V E   C H E R U N D O L O O O T
S S I   O F R A N C I S C O   T O R R E S N Z R
O R O T C E P S   N A H T A N O J R O Y R R R O
A N S A R A A R T D U C E L I   D   D U N S N E
```

185

Section 9 Vocabulary
Lesson 32

Name   **Answer Key**   Date

0209911

Vocabulary Word List		
Consolidated	Headline	Podium
Folded	Impressive	Relegated
Global	Pioneers	Tournament

Matching

Match each definition with a word.

1. **a.** A person who goes before, opening the way for others **b.** A person who does something first <u>**Pioneers**</u>	2. **a.** Assign to a lower position; reduce in rank. **b.** Expel, as if by official decree. _____
3. A platform raised above the surrounding level to give prominence to the person on it. _____	4. Cease to operate or cause to cease operating. _____
5. A sporting competition in which contestants play a series of games to decide the winner. _____	6. Remarkable, memorable, outstanding. _____
7. Relating to, or involving the whole earth or world; worldwide. _____	8. **a.** Unite into one. **b.** Forming a solid mass. _____
9. **a.** The heading or caption of a newspaper article. **b.** An attention getting sentence or pharse printed in large type across the top of a news story. _____	

Name _____ **Vocabulary** Date _____

(Answer ID # 0902816)

Select the definition that most nearly defines the given word.

1. **Global** Ⓐ Assign to a lower position; reduce in rank. Ⓑ Relating to, or involving the whole earth or world; worldwide. Ⓒ Unite into one.	2. **Tournament** Ⓐ Remarkable, memorable, outstanding. Ⓑ A sporting competition in which contestants play a series of games to decide the winner. Ⓒ A person who does something first
3. **Folded** Ⓐ Cease to operate or cause to cease operating. Ⓑ Forming a solid mass. Ⓒ Expel, as if by official decree.	4. **Impressive** Forming a solid mass. Ⓑ Remarkable, memorable, outstanding. Ⓒ Assign to a lower position; reduce in rank.
5. **Headline** Ⓐ A person who goes before, opening the way for others Ⓑ An attention getting sentence or phrase printed in large type across the top of a news story. Ⓒ Relating to, or involving the whole earth or world; worldwide.	6. **Podium** Ⓐ The heading or caption of a newspaper article. Ⓑ A person who goes before, opening the way for others Ⓒ A platform raised above the surrounding level to give prominence to the person on it.
7. **Pioneers** Ⓐ Cease to operate or cause to cease operating. Ⓑ Assign to a lower position; reduce in rank. Ⓒ A person who goes before, opening the way for others	8. **Relegated** Ⓐ A sporting competition in which contestants play a series of games to decide the winner. Ⓑ An attention getting sentence or phrase printed in large type across the top of a news story. Ⓒ Expel, as if by official decree.

Vocabulary: History of Soccer in the United States

Word List		
Consolidated	Headline	Podium
Folded	Impressive	Relegated
Global	Pioneers	Tournament

Definitions

Consolidated (kuhnsoluhdaytuhd) *adjective, verb*
1. Unite into one.
2. Forming a solid mass.

Folded (fohlduhd)
Cease to operate or cause to cease operating.

Global (glohbuhl) *adjective*
Relating to, or involving the whole earth or world; worldwide.
Synonyms: ecumenical, comprehensive, universal, cosmopolitan
Antonym: parochial

Headline (hEHdliin) *noun, verb*
1. The heading or caption of a newspaper article.
2. An attention getting sentence or phrase printed in large type across the top of a news story.

Impressive (ihmprEHsihv) *adjective*
Remarkable, memorable, outstanding.
Synonyms: awesome, luxurious, influential, gorgeous, moving, poignant, touching, affecting, stirring
Antonyms: unimpressive, ordinary, feeble, tame, weak

Pioneers (piiuhnihrz) *verb*
1. A person who goes before, opening the way for others
2. A person who does something first
    FIFA was birthed in 1904 and the first FIFA World Cup was held in 1930. United States is one of the pioneers to play soccer as a national sport. Back in the early

189

18th century.

Podium   (pohdeeuhm) *noun*

 A platform raised above the surrounding level to give prominence to the person on it.

> In the 1930 FIFA World Cup, Team USA finished on the podium behind Uruguay, the eventual champions and Brazil, runner up

Relegated   (rEHluhgaytihd)

1. Assign to a lower position; reduce in rank.
2. Expel, as if by official decree.

Tournament   (turnuhmuhnt) *noun*

 A sporting competition in which contestants play a series of games to decide the winner.

Synonyms: games, challenge, meet, series, competition, match, contest

References

1. BBC Sports News: http://www.bbc.co.uk
2. Edhelper: http://www.edhelper.com/
3. Fédération Internationale de Football Association (FIFA): http://www.fifa.com/
4. Wikipedia: http://en.wikipedia.org.

Other References

5 Baseball-reference: History of baseball in United States http://www.baseball-reference.com. Retrieved April 2, 2011
6. Ehow: The History of Basketball in the USA: http://www.ehow.com/about_6707325_history-basketball-usa.html Retrieved April 2, 2011
7. Betterbasketball: The History of Basketball in the USA http://www.betterbasketball.com/history-of-basketball/ Retrieved April 2, 2011
8. Google: History of basketball http://www.google.com. Retrieved April 2, 2011
9 Soccer-for-Parents: US soccer history http://www.soccer-for-parents.com/us-soccer-history.html#origin. Retrieved   March 31, 2011